INTELLIGENT LEADERSHIP

INTELLIGENT LEADERSHIP

WHAT YOU NEED TO KNOW TO UNLOCK YOUR FULL POTENTIAL

JOHN MATTONE

American Management Association

New York • Atlanta • Brussels • Chicago • Mexico City • San Francisco
Shanghai • Tokyo • Toronto • Washington, D. C.

Bulk discounts available. For details visit:
www.amacombooks.org/go/specialsales
Or contact special sales:
Phone: 800-250-5308
E-mail: specialsls@amanet.org
View all the AMACOM titles at: www.amacombooks.org
American Management Association: www.amanet.org

This publication is designed to provide accurate and authoritative information in regard to the subject matter covered. It is sold with the understanding that the publisher is not engaged in rendering legal, accounting, or other professional service. If legal advice or other expert assistance is required, the services of a competent professional person should be sought.

Library of Congress Cataloging-in-Publication Data

Mattone, John.
    Intelligent leadership: what you need to know to unlock your full
    potential / John Mattone.
        p. cm.
    Includes bibliographical references and index.
    ISBN: 978-0-8144-3237-2 (hardc)
    ISBN: 978-0-8144-3937-1 (pbk)
    ISBN: 978-0-8144-3238-9 (ebook)
    1. Leadership. 2. Executive ability. I. Title.
    HD57.7.M3537 2013
    658.4'092—dc23   2012040459

About AMA
American Management Association (www.amanet.org) is a world leader in talent development, advancing the skills of individuals to drive business success. Our mission is to support the goals of individuals and organizations through a complete range of products and services, including classroom and virtual seminars, webcasts, webinars, podcasts, conferences, corporate and government solutions, business books, and research. AMA's approach to improving performance combines experiential learning—learning through doing—with opportunities for ongoing professional growth at every step of one's career journey.

Printing number

10 9 8 7 6 5 4 3 2 1

CONTENTS

CHAPTER 6:

**Understanding Your Entertainer
Leadership Trait**.......................................**79**

CHAPTER 7:

**Understanding Your Artist
Leadership Trait**...**89**

CHAPTER 8:

**Understanding Your Thinker
Leadership Trait**..**99**

CHAPTER 9:

**Understanding Your Disciple
Leadership Trait**...**109**

CHAPTER 10:

CHAPTER 11:

CHAPTER 12:

CHAPTER 13:

FOREWORD

With *Intelligent Leadership*, John Mattone taps into his years of experience to help leaders become the best leaders they can be. This work is a valiant effort toward that cause! Based on his *Map of Leadership Maturity*, John focuses on integrating a leader's inner strength and outer competencies as the key to leadership success even in today's environment of enormous challenge and global change.

John understands that ultimately leaders' actions say much more to employees and customers about their leadership skills than mere words ever can. Companies have wasted millions of dollars and countless hours agonizing over the wording of statements that are inscribed on plaques and hung over office watercoolers. These pronouncements, however, do not change people's behavior. Companies that do the best job of living up to their values and developing ethical employees, including managers, recognize that the real cause of success—or failure—is always the people, not the words.

John provides three unique tools for leaders who want to unleash their potential: his Wheel of Intelligent Leadership™, his Map of Leadership Maturity™ (The Map), and the Leadership Enneagram Inventory. Using these tools, leaders learn about their own personality style and leadership maturity level, as well as how to lead people of different style types. These tools will help leaders who want to unlock their potential!

As you embark on your leadership journey, one bit of advice: Change is hard. It often takes longer than you think, and it can be difficult. Don't just read

John's book; put it into practice. Pick up the tools he offers, and take personal ownership of your success. Remember, real change is not a one-time thing, and it requires real effort. Being an authentic leader, both inside and out, is a lifetime pursuit!

Life is good.

Marshall Goldsmith

Marshall Goldsmith was recently recognized as the world's most influential leadership thinker in the biannual Thinkers50 study, sponsored by the *Harvard Business Review*. His 31 books include the *New York Times* bestsellers *MOJO* and *What Got You Here Won't Get You There*.

ACKNOWLEDGMENTS

This book was truly a team effort. I want to thank my incredible wife of 34 years, Gayle, who has stood by me every step of the way. Gayle is the most courageous individual I have ever known. She is a two-time breast cancer survivor who never gave up on life and who persevered and continues to persevere to help others through her work as a registered nurse. Gayle is a remarkable role model for our entire family. Gayle, I love you.

Our four children—Jared, 30; Nick, 27; Kristina, 23; and Matt, 20—your love is my strength. I love you. I want to thank my father-in-law, Mr. Bill O'Halloran, for his many years of support and love and for giving me the gift of his daughter Gayle. I want to thank my late parents, Dominic and Jane Mattone, and my late mother-in-law, Jean O'Halloran, who I know looks down on me and my family. I want to thank by brothers-in-law, Dr. John O'Halloran, a truly gifted sports medicine expert, Michael O'Halloran, a talented professor of management at Bentley University, and Paul O'Halloran, one of the top high school basketball coaches in America. More than anything, these men are great fathers and husbands. We go forward every day with character, conviction, and confidence beneath our wings.

I want to thank all my clients and participants who have attended my speeches and programs and those whom I have had the privilege to coach throughout the years. I have learned so much from you, and I want to thank you for your contributions to this book. I especially want to thank Jan Jones from Jan Jones Worldwide Speakers Bureau, who is my friend and manager. I must thank my good friends Jill Gallagher, Rich Longhurst, and Steve Anastasio from Navy Federal Credit Union—thanks for everything. Special thanks also to Bill Logue, CEO of FedEx Freight, and to Sheila Harrell, Vice President, Customer Service Operations, FedEx TechConnect, both of whom are close friends and incredible business leaders. I want to thank Steve Francis, Charl Butler, and the entire team at AgFirst Farm Credit Bank for being great friends and colleagues. I also have to thank John Plunkett from Cobb Energy and Melanie Polonofsky from BASF.

Thanks go to my close friends and business partners—Bonnie Hagemann, CEO; Annette White-Klososky, partner; and Dawn Ciarlone, Director of Operations of Executive Development Associates and the entire EDA team; Jim Higgins, Ron Gross, Carla Higgins, and the entire Mercer consulting team; Cabot Jaffee Sr., Cabot Jaffee, and Glen Jaffee from AlignMark; Vegar Wiik, Sybil Alfred, Natalya Sabga, Debra Delach-Dodd, and the entire team from Florida Atlantic University's Executive Education Department; Elaine Eisenman and Joe Weintraub from Babson College's Executive Education team; Tony Colao, founder of MasterMedia Speakers Bureau; and especially Berthony Poux, Mark Goldberg, Morsell Allison, and the entire Talent Management Alliance team. I want to extend special thanks to Des Dearlove and Stuart Crainer from the Thinkers50 for their belief in me and my work. Thanks go to Dan Hoeyer, CEO of Business Educators, for his support. And, of course, I want to thank all our speaker bureau partners for their support as well. Thanks are due to all my executive MBA students at Florida Atlantic University. I want to extend a special thank-you to my good friend and personal coach, Linda Mattia Potts, who has given me many gifts along the way, but the ones I most cherish are her honesty, wisdom, and inspiration.

I want to thank my colleagues Clayton Christensen and Jim Collins for their professional support and their belief in me. Special thanks go out to my friend, colleague, and close advisor, Dr. Marshall Goldsmith, who is recognized worldwide as the number one leadership thinker and expert in the field. Marshall, thanks for your guidance, support, and friendship.

Lastly, this project would not have been possible without the outstanding efforts of editor Christina Parisi, Michael Sivilli, and the entire AMACOM team, as well as the copyediting work of Fred Dahl. Thank you very much.

INTRODUCTION

In today's business environment, leaders at all levels are facing enormous challenges in achieving and sustaining breakthrough operating results. Globalization, economic change, toughened regulation, and tightened governance make realizing shareholder value increasingly difficult.

Intelligent Leadership is written for current and emerging leaders who are striving to break through their self-imposed limiting thoughts, emotions, and habits so that they can seize control of their leadership destiny. The book is for the leaders and future leaders who want to become more effective, strategic, operationally focused, and balanced. It is for the leaders and future leaders who are energized and passionate about becoming the very best leaders they can be. More than anything, *Intelligent Leadership* is for leaders and emerging leaders who recognize that *preparation* is the key to unlocking and seizing the massive leadership opportunities that are beginning to present themselves in every industry, every business, and just about every country worldwide. This book will prepare and cultivate your heart, mind, and soul so that you are poised to touch the hearts, minds, and souls of those with whom you work. In the role of leader, you have no more noble, worthy, or rewarding pursuit than unlocking and unleashing greatness in yourself, your employees, and your teams.

Intelligent Leadership is research and empirically based. The book uses my Wheel of Intelligent Leadership™ and Map of Leadership Maturity™ as the foundation for explaining the predictive relationships between what I call a leader's inner-core strength (character, values, positive beliefs, positive emotions, self-concept) and outer core (i.e., leadership) competencies, ultimate leadership success, and organizational effectiveness. The contents will challenge you to reflect on, connect with, and accept both *your* leadership strengths and development opportunities. From there, the book will guide you in specific ways on how to strengthen your inner-core character, values, beliefs, thoughts, and emotions, as well as your outer-core competencies, so that you can break through your self-imposed limitations and achieve all you are capable of achieving as a leader and as a person.

This book contains the best of what I have learned in my 30 years as a human capital consultant, executive coach, and industrial psychologist. I have included a number of best practices, case study examples, authoritative research, practical assessments, as well as a variety of practical tools and models to equip you—the leader or emerging leader—with the knowledge, skills, and passion to become the absolute best leader you can be.

This book originated from four sources:
1. My experiences from traveling all over the globe for the last 30 years
2. Research I have conducted and continue to conduct on trends in talent management and executive development
3. Consulting with over 250 organizations
4. Coaching over 200 executives

My speaking, consulting, and executive coaching work has put me in contact with many types of organizations and people around the world. I listened, observed, and gave assistance when and where needed. This book reflects the essence of what I learned about how leaders and emerging leaders can become the absolute best leaders they can be.

INTELLIGENT LEADERSHIP

CHAPTER

1

Your Leadership Success Roadmap

In a breakthrough *executive trends* global research study that I conducted with my colleague, Bonnie Hagemann, we clearly confirmed that *identifying and developing high-potential and emerging leaders* is and will continue to be one of the top business issues facing CEOs. In most organizations, 40 to 70 percent of all executives will become eligible for retirement in the next five years.

In our increasingly knowledge-driven world economy, organizations are right to fear this imminent brain drain, suspecting that, when executives leave the firm, business may follow. Yet high-potentials and emerging leaders—those most likely to rise to fill those highest positions—account for less than 8 to 10 percent of the talent pool. That's in the United States. In other countries, like Canada, Australia, the United Kingdom, Japan, and China, and in just about every country except India and various countries in Africa and South America, this issue is as pronounced as it is in the United States, if not more so. Therefore, identifying, developing, and retaining such rare talent truly is a mission-critical *global* challenge for CEOs, senior executives, managers, and HR directors.

Given this indisputable global business challenge, the implication for current and emerging leaders is clear: The demand for outstanding leaders will soon surpass the current supply, and therefore, if you are a current leader or emerging leader, you will be able to capitalize on substantial opportunities if you are poised and ready. In your own ascent up the ladder, you can be certain that all organizations will be asking more of their leaders; expectations, demands, and pressure will only increase, not decrease. The demand for truly outstanding leaders has never been higher, and organizations are raising the bar—as they must—in order to compete successfully on the global stage.

Where Are the Outstanding Business Leaders?

As I travel the globe, meeting with senior executive teams, coaching executives, and speaking to various management groups, it is clear to me that the world of business has very few outstanding leaders. There are many very good leaders. The distribution of outstanding leadership, like anything else, follows the shape of a bell-shaped curve. I always knew this. Everyone has always known this. But nobody really cared because being a good leader has always been good enough to keep a position and meet its basic requirements. But things are changing quickly. The bell-shaped curve needs to be shaped into a negatively skewed distribution, in which all organizations possess a larger percentage of very good and outstanding leaders just to be able to compete.

I had suspected the need for this critical shift for a couple of years, but it became very clear in 2011 as we were interviewing executives as part of our *Trends in Executive Development Research Study* (Pearson, 2011). Beyond the actual research, an interesting qualitative note emerged. When I ask executives to identify a great leader in their lives—someone who had a positive impact on them and helped shape their values—roughly 9 times out of 10, they mention a former teacher, coach, parent, grandparent, or friend, as opposed to a business leader. Unfortunately, the fact is that most of us in the business world can identify the poor managers we have had much more quickly than we can the great ones. Why is this?

There is no clear answer; however, it is pretty clear that many managers are promoted before they are ready to assume leadership roles. They are not adequately trained, coached, and mentored by more seasoned executives, who often can share stories and insights to dramatically shorten a manager's learning curve. More than anything else, I believe the speed and pace of change in business—technology shifts, demographic shifts, and a more demanding operating environment—present daunting challenges to most leaders. Frankly, very few possess both the strong inner core of values, character, beliefs, thoughts, and emotions and the set of outer-core leadership competencies that are truly required to successfully overcome these challenges. In the end, too many executives are beginning to derail or have already derailed because of character flaws or perhaps just sheer immaturity.

Let's look at a couple of real-world examples of outstanding leadership.

The Role Models of Outstanding Leadership

Two CEOs (one current and one former) are recognized worldwide as leaders who possess strong character, a strong inner core, and superlative leadership skills. The current CEO of Amazon.com, Jeff Bezos, founded his company in 1994 as an online bookstore. Bezos has built Amazon into the largest retailer on the Web, selling everything from groceries to electronics to shoes. Amazon consistently succeeds with risky new ventures, a success that Bezos credits to tenacity and obsession with customer needs. Excerpts from an interview in *U.S. News & World Report,* which David LaGesse conducted with Bezos in 2011, contained numerous examples of his strong inner core (i.e., character, values, positive beliefs, positive emotions, self-concept) and outer core (i.e., leadership competencies) that, together, form the foundation of what I refer to as *leadership maturity.*

When Bezos was asked about the need for a long-term view, he replied:

> My own view is that every company needs a long-term view. If you're going to take a long-term orientation, you have to be willing to stay "heads down" and ignore a wide array of critics, even well-meaning critics. If you don't have a willingness to be misunderstood for a long period of time, then you can't have a long-term orientation. Because we have done it many times and have come out the other side, we have enough internal stories that we can tell ourselves. While we're crossing the desert, we may be thirsty, but we sincerely believe there's an oasis on the other side.

In this answer, Bezos reveals numerous examples of his leadership maturity:

- Strong statements of conviction;
- Character elements of diligence and focus
- The ability to handle uncertainty and ambiguity
- An understanding of the value of experience and "references" that are the foundation for creating strong and compelling beliefs about what is possible
- A powerful sense of optimism

Another great example of outstanding leadership is Anne Mulcahy, former CEO of Xerox. When Mulcahy took over Xerox in 2000, she delivered a blunt message to shareholders: "Xerox's business model is unsustainable. Expenses are too high and profit margins too low to return to profitability." Shareholders, wanting easy answers to complex problems, started to dump their shares, which drove Xerox's stock price down 26 percent the next day. Looking back on that dark time, Mulcahy admitted she could have been more tactful; however, she had decided it would be more credible and authoritative if she had acknowledged that the company was broken and that dramatic actions were needed to fix it.

Although she had been with Xerox for 25 years and knew the company well, when Mulcahy was named CEO, she acknowledged her lack of financial expertise. She quickly enlisted the treasurer's office to tutor her in the fine points of finance before meeting with the company's bankers. Her advisors told her to file for bankruptcy to clear $18 billion in debt, but Mulcahy resisted, telling them, "Bankruptcy is never a win." In fact, Mulcahy thought that using bankruptcy to escape debt would make it more difficult in the future for Xerox to compete seriously as a high-tech player. Instead, she chose a much more difficult and risky goal: "restoring Xerox to a great company again." To gain support from Xerox's leadership team, she met personally with the top 100 executives. She let them know honestly how dire the situation was and asked them whether they were ready to commit. A full 98 out of 100 decided to stay, and the bulk of them are still with the company today.

Like Bezos, Mulcahy's actions reflect numerous examples of her *executive maturity*:

- Character elements of honesty, modesty, humility, and courage
- A powerful sense of vision
- Skill at empowering others
- Her passion, drive, and incredible zeal

THE OTHER END OF THE CONTINUUM: UNLEADERLIKE CHARACTER AND BEHAVIOR

Scott Thompson is now the ex-CEO of Yahoo, Inc. One day, he was sitting on top of the world with a $1-million salary and $5.5 million in stock options. The next day, his board asked him to resign in shame and embarrassment for lying about a degree he said he had earned in the early 1980s from Stonehill College in Massachusetts. A few years ago, Dennis Kozlowski, then CEO of mammoth

Tyco, was also asked to resign amid strong speculation he was siphoning company money for his personal use. The courts later determined that Kozlowski indeed saw Tyco's checking account as an extension of his personal checking account to the tune of over $80 million. Kozlowski is currently in jail in a New York State correctional facility.

These are just two examples of extreme *leadership immaturity*. Character flaws clearly drove this unleaderlike and unquestioned illegal behavior. There are other numerous examples—executives, CEOs, senior executives, managers, and emerging executives (some of whom I have coached) who were skyrocketing one day and falling from grace the next. When character is involved—even the question of character—my experience is that the executive may never recover. When executives reach the pinnacle and then suddenly plummet, there are no limbs to break their fall; their drop is as swift as it is unforgiving.

One of the messages I deliver to executives when I coach them is this: *Character doesn't determine your destiny; it determines your ultimate destiny.* Your character, or the lack of it, will strongly impact how you are viewed and talked about, and it ultimately determines how others will remember you. All of us retain total control over how we will be remembered. It is a conscious choice we make. The question I ask all executives is, *"Will you make the right choice?"*

AMANT'S DEFINITION OF CHARACTER

I am privileged to speak all over the globe to a variety of leadership audiences. Speaking is one of the great joys in my life. On occasion, close friends ask me to address a sports team, high school seniors, or middle school eighth-graders. I am honored to be asked because I love to connect with younger people in the hope that my message will have a positive impact on them as they grow and mature.

A close friend, Judy, who is the principal of a large middle school in greater Orlando, Florida, once asked me to address their 500 graduating eighth-graders along with their parents, grandparents, and friends—about 2,000 people in all. Judy wanted me to speak primarily to the young graduates about leadership and success. I was excited about the opportunity to share my thoughts on the topic of character as a key in driving our success and our ultimate destiny.

Following a wonderful introduction by Judy, I stood before the 500 graduates, prepared to share my own definition of character (more on this later). Then I decided to pose the question, "Does anyone want to propose a great definition of character?" After three or four seconds, a young man put his hand up. I asked him if he wanted to share a definition of character, and he softly muttered some powerful words that only a few of his classmates and I could hear. His words so impressed me that I asked him his name and he said, "Amant." I then asked him if he would share his definition with everyone (this time using the microphone). "Yes," he replied.

"Parents, grandparents, friends, everyone," I announced, "Amant would like to share his definition of character." With that, I turned the microphone over to him. Amant stood up and with pride, clarity, and eloquence, stated, "Character is what you do when no one else is watching." The crowd erupted in applause. I was awestruck, not because I had never heard this definition, but rather because of Amant's clarity, conviction, and eloquence in sharing this powerful definition. It moved me and the thousands of people in attendance. Clearly, this young man recognized the incredible value of possessing a working definition of character as a guide to his everyday decision making. I went on to predict a great future for Amant and for all the graduates as long as they continue to use their strength of character as a foundation and guide to their everyday decisions.

IDENTIFYING HIGH-POTENTIAL LEADERS

Senior executive teams often ask me what they should look for in identifying their high-potential leaders. My answer is always clear: They need to look for people who possess both a strong inner-core and a strong outer-core set of competencies, which enable them to demonstrate the *capability* to develop, grow, and self-nurture to the level required for success at the most senior executive levels. The most critical thing to look for and measure, however, is character.

The essence of character is undoubtedly multifaceted and complex. When working with executives who possess character, I see a lot of what we see in Jeff Bezos and Ann Mulcahy. When working with organizations to help them identify their high-potential and emerging leaders, I look for evidence that they are, at a minimum, *courageous*. I look for leaders who have the guts to make the tough but ethical decisions. I look for their willingness to sometimes stand alone, in the teeth of pressure (possibly even from their own managers) to go in a counter, sometimes less ethical direction. When coaching executives, I explain that saying no to the easiest and most rewarding route, when that decision doesn't align with what you know is the correct one, may seem difficult. However, as soon as you begin flirting with such decisions—those that yield better operating results, greater revenue, and greater profits yet clearly compromise you ethically and morally—you enter a world of agony and stress. Making such choices will lead you into a world of painful long-term consequences, not the least of which is an increased probability you will say yes to more insidious acts in time. This is exactly what happened to Dennis Kozlowski. Great leaders—truly great leaders—have the courage to make the right decision every time.

Great leaders also possess the character elements of *diligence, gratitude, honesty, modesty,* and *loyalty* (more on these in Chapter 3).

Most Unleaderlike Behavior is Just Plain Immaturity

Leaders generally derail not because of a character flaw but rather because they respond immaturely to mounting stress and change. Leaders who are immature in their thoughts, beliefs, attitudes, and habits, however, are capable of recovering from their unleaderlike behavior, unlike the poor-character leaders in the previous section. For example, one of the most important traits of great leaders is what I call the *Helping* trait. Leaders who are selfless, giving, and altruistic are demonstrating the mature behaviors associated with the Helping trait. However, when their helping is done in an unauthentic way, with strings attached, they are demonstrating the immature behaviors associated with that trait. Great leaders also possess a mature *Disciple* trait. Leaders who can follow others and who value being part of something bigger than just themselves are demonstrating the mature behaviors of this powerful trait. When leaders demonstrate a lack of belief in themselves and do not think they are worthy of success and accolades, they are showing the immature behaviors of this trait. In later chapters, I will explain in detail the mature and immature behaviors associated with the nine critical traits that define the essence of leadership.

I have come to believe that organizations that do not compulsively develop their leaders and future leaders—through coaching, mentoring, executive development programs, action learning projects, and the like—unknowingly grow and multiply leaders with a high probability for derailment and failure. At a minimum, when an organization, leader, or future leader leaves things to chance, the probability of leader derailment or success is the same. With targeted coaching and real prescriptions for strengthening their inner and outer cores, however, leaders and future leaders can seize the considerable opportunities that await them. At the same time, they can successfully mitigate the enormous risks associated with the unrelenting pace and complexity of change they face in their part of the business world. These principles, then, become the blueprint for helping you—the leader and future leader—build a strong, compelling foundation for becoming absolutely the best leader you can be.

Let's look at the key factors and business trends that offer huge opportunities for the savvy, mature leader *and* potential derailment for the unsavvy, immature leader.

Business Challenges and Trends: Massive Opportunity or Potential Derailer?

Today, the pace of change in business is dramatically faster than in previous times. Top executives in firms today report fiercer competitive business environments and more globalized patterns of operations than ever. Technological advances continue to significantly impact both communication infrastructures and the strategic business decisions that executives make in terms of trade, resources, and competition. Future leaders will need to be savvy conceptual and strategic thinkers, to possess deep integrity and intellectual openness, to find innovative ways to create loyalty, to lead increasingly diverse and independent teams over which they may not always have direct authority, and to have the maturity to relinquish their own power in favor of creating and fostering collaborative approaches inside and outside their organizations.

To successfully develop this combination of inner- and outer-core capability, the leaders of the future will likely need to reinforce and intensify the thinking and behavior that propelled them to the top of their organizations in the first place. According to the Hay Group's Leadership 2030 Research Study, if leaders want their organizations to survive and thrive in the next 20 years, they have no choice but to dramatically shift and strengthen how they lead. If the leaders themselves want to survive and thrive, they must change how they lead. To survive the future, leaders must be capable of helping their organizations win the race of innovation, global presence, and talent.

In their breakthrough study, the Hay Group identified six megatrends that will affect organizations and their leaders profoundly over the coming decades:

- Globalization
- Scarcity of resources
- Demographic changes
- Growing freedom of choice
- The digital age
- Harnessing technology

In the following sections, I identify a few of the trends that I believe will have a dramatic impact on you—the current and emerging leader—as you strive to become the absolute best leader you can be. I sincerely hope and desire that you continue to sharpen your inner core and outer core so that you recognize and embrace these challenging trends as real opportunities. They are indeed pathways to unlocking and unleashing your massive capability and to true leadership greatness.

Unrelenting Change

When meeting and coaching executives, I hear a lot about how they view change within their organizations. Most are quick to point out that the challenges their own organization face now are much more complex than they were five years ago. "Why do you think this is true?" I ask. They talk about constant internal changes in their organizations, such as structure and process changes, as well as a myriad of external challenges, such as market volatility, talent shortages, globalization, competition, technology, cost and profitability pressure, and rising customer expectations.

Innovation Imperative

Innovation. Every organization I visit, every leader I talk to, is searching for the next big idea. This imperative pressures and challenges all leaders and all future leaders because now they must lead and participate on task forces, cross-functional teams, and participate in off-site innovation training programs. The need to excel as collaborators and mediators is no longer a nice-to-have; it is a must-have capability. In most organizations, most of the leaders and future leaders are involved in multiple innovation projects that involve searching for and implementing new products, as well as processes such as talent development initiatives, reward and recognition programs, and benchmarking projects.

It's a Virtual World

With increased globalization, my clients have to efficiently and effectively bridge geographical, cultural, and functional boundaries. I truly believe that being effective as a virtual leader is different than being effective as a face-to-face leader. The skills of communication are critical. Possessing the capability to engage in clear, consistent, and frequent communication using a variety of collaborative technologies will continue to be important skills for all leaders and future leaders. Of course, firmly embedded in the skill of effective communication are the inner-core elements of character, honesty, and integrity.

It's a Velcro World

Great leaders are able to velcro their people and teams to their mission, vision, and strategies. This ability will continue to be a challenge as people's careers play an increasingly important role in their quest for self-fulfillment. Generation X and Y people crave greater convergence between their personal and professional lives. They demand recognition, self-development opportunities, and work/life balance; more than anything, they want to be engaged in their work and careers. Leaders and future leaders, given these changing demographics, will need to be diligent and passionate about generating personal loyalty among their people by building relationships with them based on rapport, trust, and credibility. Clearly, leaders who have strong inner and outer cores will be able to velcro their people and teams to them and to their vision, mission, and direction.

THE ROADMAP CONTINUES

Chapter 2 of this book begins with my explanation of a leader's outer-core strategic and tactical competencies. You will preview the Strategic-Tactical Leadership Index™ (STLI™), a leadership assessment that I use in my executive coaching work to determine a leader's current performance on the nine competencies comprising their outer core. The STLI™ isolates a leader's most effective competencies, as well as the competencies that need to be developed. You will find the STLI™ in Appendix A. You should complete the STLI™ as a self-assessment after you have read Chapter 2 or after you have finished reading the book. The STLI™ is also used in a multirater format, in which leaders obtain feedback from their employees, peers, manager, and other key stakeholders. A multirater survey is a critical component of my executive coaching work. So, although you will gain value in completing the STLI™ as a self-assessment, you will derive more value by reaching out to your stakeholders and asking them to complete the STLI™ as well.

Chapter 3 will provide you with the opportunity to explore and learn more about your inner core. The body of leadership research is rich with theory about whether leaders are born with innate leadership skills or whether those skills and abilities are the result of training, experience, and repetitive application. The answer is that both are true. Your inner core consists of your thoughts, values, and belief systems coupled with unique experiences and something I call your *reference reservoir*. In combination, these elements comprise your self-concept, and they drive your interpretation of events and facts, your emotions, your behaviors, and your ultimate results as a leader.

Also residing within your inner core are your elements of character and values. Your *character* consists of multifaceted elements, which ultimately play out in what you believe, what you do, and what you decide. You will learn that your character determines your ultimate destiny. When reading Chapter 3, take the time to consciously reflect on your values and experiences and recognize how these two elements impact the quality of your decisions. Going through this exercise will enable you to make more positive, meaningful decisions that result in greater individual and organizational success. At the same time, you will learn to insulate yourself from bias and the temptation to resort to unethical choices in an effort to win at all costs. As we head for heightened turbulence due to increased globalization and technological advances, my personal mandate to you is to dive in and thoroughly examine the strength and vibrancy of your inner core.

The remaining chapters in this book will introduce to you the *Map of Leadership Maturity*, a powerful tool that provides you with the framework and roadmap for exploring and distinguishing between the nine distinct predominant traits defining great leadership. The Map is a powerful tool for helping you—the leader or future leader, regardless of level. It helps you gain a granular understanding of the degree of maturity that you exhibit in the values, thoughts, emotions, and behaviors of your own predominant trait, as well as in the other eight traits that comprise your unique leadership fingerprint. You will learn that being a successful leader is less a function of your predominant trait and much more a function of the relative maturity with which you evidence your predominant trait—and each of your other eight traits. You will learn specific strategies on how you can strengthen your maturity within all your traits. You will learn specific strategies for building rapport, trust, and credibility with individuals who present a different predominant trait than yours. In addition to learning key insights about their leadership styles, you will build your knowledge and skills so that you can more successfully lead different style types. Ultimately, in writing this book, my sincere desire is that you begin to recognize, appreciate, and internalize that unlocking and unleashing your own leadership potential is a function of your possessing a passionate and diligent desire to:

1. Discover your own unique development goals and strategic developmental pathways.
2. Begin executing these strategies with passion and focus.
3. Learn and course-correct continuously as you execute with passion and focus.

Enjoy the journey. I am confident you will find it to be the most rewarding professional and personal journey you have ever taken.

Using the Appendixes

- *Appendix A: The Strategic-Tactical Leadership Index™ Survey:* Please complete the STLI™ after reading Chapter 2 or, better, after reading the entire book. Although you will gain value completing the STLI™ as a self-assessment, more value can be gained by reaching out to key stakeholders and asking them to complete the assessment as well.
- *Appendix B: The STLI™ Developmental Strategies:* This appendix includes a number of developmental strategies associated with the nine competencies comprising the STLI™. Many of these strategies you will find helpful as you prepare your customized Individual Development Plan (IDP).
- *Appendix C: The Mattone Leadership Enneagram Inventory (MLEI):* This section contains the MLEI, detailed scoring instructions, and a brief interpretive guide. Please complete the MLEI after you have read the book and ideally at about the same time you complete the STLI™. Your assessment results from both the STLI™ and MLEI will provide you with a valid picture of the strength of your inner core and outer core, which you can now leverage in building your customized IDP.
- *Appendix D: Assessment-Driven Individual Development Plan:* This section will provide a detailed six-step process for building your custom IDP by integrating your assessment results with how your current performance is perceived by you and possibly by your stakeholders. Ultimately, you will uncover your indisputable and surprise strengths as well as your indisputable and surprise development needs. This becomes the foundation for creating a powerful IDP.
- *Appendix E: Sample Leadership Individual Development Plan:* This section contains a sample IDP.

CHAPTER

2

The Wheel of Intelligent Leadership™: The Outer Core

As the "3C" Pyramid in Exhibit 2.1 illustrates, the foundation to unlocking and unleashing your executive potential consists of your leadership capability, commitment, and connectedness.

- Leadership *capability* refers to your present skills and competencies that can be developed, nourished, and enhanced. Think of your leadership capability as can-do, which is very different from what you are currently doing.
- Leadership *commitment* refers to the motivational factors that drive you to become the best leader possible (i.e., your passion, drive, motivation, and zeal). Think of your leadership as will-do.
- Finally, leadership *connectedness* has both internal and external

EXHIBIT 2.1:   **THE 3C PYRAMID**

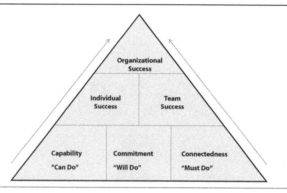

focuses. Internally, great leaders possess a set of values and character elements that are aligned with those values and character elements that drive success in leaders (more on this in Chapter 3). Externally, great leaders are truly aligned and connected to the mission, values, and goals of their organization. Think of your leadership connectedness as must-do.

Your can-do, will-do, and must-do as a leader or emerging leader are the critical foundational pieces for creating your own blueprint not only for success but also for driving both team and organizational success. To use an economics analogy, your can-do, will-do, and must-do are the leading indicators in predicting your leadership success and the operating success of your organization. If you possess, develop, and execute all three leading indicators, then you and your organization will flourish. Your leadership successes will be evident not only in your individual contributions but also in the contributions of your teams.

Leaders—truly great leaders—continuously commit to strengthening their own can-do, will-do, and must-do. However, also critical is recognizing the irrefutable connection between leaders' actually freely choosing to commit to continuous improvement and the resulting impact of this free choice decision on their employees and team. Ultimately, under the umbrella of their own ever improving capability, great leaders create powerful, engaging cultures in which their people and teams make the free choice to commit to continuous improvement and a real drive to become the best they can be, both individually and collectively. The pathway to unlocking and unleashing greatness in individuals and teams is through the leaders and their commitment to monitoring, calibrating, improving, developing, and strengthening their own can-do, will-do, and must-do. Think of organizations and teams that consistently win. They are made up of individuals (and teams), from the top leader to the lowest-level individual contributors, who show up every day saying, "I can. I will. I must" (or, "We can. We will. We must") execute at a higher level today than yesterday.

Unfortunately, there are many misconceptions about what leadership is or is not. One of the most significant misconceptions is that every great leader is born to lead. In fact, some leaders—the minority—were born with the right DNA, make-up, and characteristics. Because of the gifts bestowed on them, they demonstrate a clear predisposition to becoming great leaders, notwithstanding the effects of family and culture. Some leaders simply have "the right stuff" and have always had it.

That said, the vast majority of great leaders—over 95 percent—have become great leaders through personal choice. The evidence of great leadership is that of a leader who has made a conscious decision to execute the can-do, will-do, and must-do and commit to never-ending improvement. The notion of calibration-development-recalibration is exceptionally powerful. We see this concept of learning agility repeatedly in learning organizations and other top firms that have developed great leaders.

All great leaders need to have a very clear mental picture of what capability, commitment, and alignment constitute. All great leaders need to know exactly what that picture looks like for themselves in their particular organizations. The notion that the definition of a target of leadership success is different for every leader and organization led to the explosion of competency-modeling work, primarily in the 1980s and early 1990s. Every organization was creating its own targets of leadership success. Of course, this led to the rise of consulting and research firms who took advantage of real market needs to help these organizations research and define leadership success in their own unique organization for their own unique leaders. The result? We have learned that the definition of leadership success—the leadership success target comprised of leadership can-do, will-do, and must-do—is really not all that unique to a particular leader or organization. In the process, through years of research, we have gained tremendous intelligence about leadership success and the competencies that define success. The early leadership competency work done by David McLeland and McBer and Company, as well as the more recent work of the Center for Creative Leadership, John Kotter, Lominger, my own firm, and hundreds of other notable researchers and leading thinkers, has added not only a unique perspective but also a corroborative perspective that there is value in creating a universal target of leadership success. In Exhibit 2.2, you will see the Wheel of Intelligent Leadership™, a universal target of leadership success that is not particularly unique in some respects but truly unique in others.

The *outer core* consists of the nine strategic and tactical leadership competencies and skills you must possess to be successful as a leader now and in the future:

1. Critical thinking
2. Decision making
3. Strategic thinking
4. Emotional leadership
5. Communication skills
6. Talent leadership
7. Team leadership
8. Change leadership
9. Drive for results

The *inner core* consists of the intrapersonal and interpersonal elements that strongly impact how effectively you acquire and cultivate the nine outer-core leadership competencies. Usually, people see, experience, and pass judgment on your outer core. The inner core, though critical in driving the outer core,

EXHIBIT 2.2:   **JOHN MATTONE'S WHEEL OF INTELLIGENT LEADERSHIP™**

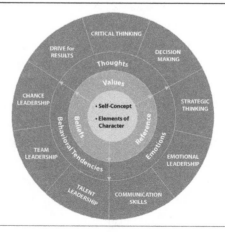

is hidden. People don't observe your self-image, beliefs and references. They observe only your behavior. In Appendix A, you will find a self-assessment (the Strategic-Tactical Leadership Index™) that enables you to assess how effectively you believe you execute the critical behaviors associated with each competency. In addition to your own self-assessment, ask your manager and other key stakeholders for their assessments of your behaviors. At a minimum, however, you will find tremendous value in working through this assessment. Appendix B contains a number of specific developmental strategies tied to the various competencies. You will find these helpful as you begin to think about how you can begin to strengthen those competencies that are your strengths and gifts, as well as those that reflect development needs.

Predictive relationships exist between your inner and outer core. If you possess a strong inner core, you have a heightened capability to acquire, grow, develop, and mature in the development and evidence of the competencies and skills comprising the outer core. The predictive connections between the inner and outer cores are shown in Exhibit 2.3.

The Wheel of Intelligent Leadership™ is unique in that no other current leadership competency models describe and detail these predictive relationships and the power of the inner-/outer-core connections in driving superior

EXHIBIT 2.3: **PREDICTIVE CONNECTIONS**

Self-Concept and Character
(values, beliefs, and references)

Thoughts

Emotions

Behavioral Tendencies

Tactical Skills/Strategic Competencies

Results

Self-Concept and Character

leadership. The Wheel of Intelligent Leadership™ has clear implications for how you, as the leader or emerging leader, can best calibrate and recalibrate your inner and outer cores. Once you understand your inner and outer cores (as well as their complex interactions) and you learn how each core (and complex interaction) truly drives and shapes your behavior and the outcomes you experience as a leader, you will be better equipped to successfully navigate the challenges and trends discussed in Chapter 1.

The Wheel of Intelligent Leadership™ is a powerful blueprint for all leaders and emerging leaders who are looking for conceptual understanding, intellectual guidance, and detailed prescriptions for unlocking and unleashing their leadership potential and greatness. It gives answers. In my coaching work, some leaders are willing to dive into understanding their head, heart, and soul, to be totally introspective and honest, to be totally objective about the strength and vibrancy of both their inner and outer cores, and to enjoy a significantly higher chance of achieving greatness as leaders in their professional and personal lives.

The nine strategic and tactical leadership competencies are discussed next. Along the way, I provide significant detail about what each competency is and how best you can execute each competency. The inner core is discussed in the next chapter.

THE NINE OUTER-CORE STRATEGIC COMPETENCIES

Critical Thinking

The first of the nine outer-core competencies is *critical thinking* (Exhibit 2.4). The word *thinking* can describe any number of mental activities. Much of your natural thinking as a leader, when left unchecked, is biased, distorted, partial, uninformed, or downright prejudiced. Your effectiveness as a leader, however, depends precisely on the quality of your thoughts. *Critical thinking* is that mode of thinking, about any given subject, in which you, the thinker, improve the quality of your thinking by skillfully taking charge of its very structures and imposing intellectual standards upon them. Effective critical thinking, however, involves consideration of the full range of possibilities to a problem, including emotional, cognitive, intellectual, and psychological factors.

Shallow thinking is costly, in terms of both money and quality of life. Successful leaders are able to apply what they know to the challenges of their work.

EXHIBIT 2.4:   **CRITICAL THINKING**

All organizations today are not interested in hiring and retaining walking encyclopedias; rather, they require leaders who are independent decision makers and problem solvers and who can model this behavior to their people and teams.

Based on the pioneering work of Pearson Education, a strong critical thinker practices RED, that is:

- *R*ecognizes assumptions.
- *E*valuates arguments.
- *D*raws conclusions.

Two recent studies identified critical thinking as the number one skill of increasing importance for current and emerging leaders who are involved in businesses today. One study in particular, *The Trends in Executive Development Research Study* (Pearson, 2011). which I conducted with my colleague Bonnie Hagemann of EDA. was most compelling: *We personally interviewed and surveyed 150 human resources executives; they estimated from 1 to 28 percent of the current leaders in their own organization demonstrated "excellent" critical thinking skills.*

Authoritative research clearly connects leaders' and emerging leaders' critical thinking capability with their achieving higher-level performance and realizing their potential, combined with the realization that business will be more complex tomorrow than it is today. This finding makes this element perhaps the most pivotal leadership element for leaders, future leaders, and organizations as they strive to become the best they can be. Simply put, your ability to make sound decisions, problem-solve, plan, and implement, as well as to execute sound strategic thinking, is entirely based on possessing superior critical thinking (i.e., RED).

- *Recognizing Assumptions:* Assumptions are statements that are implied to be true in the absence of proof. Identifying assumptions helps in the discovery of information gaps and enriches views of issues. Assumptions can be unstated or directly stated. The ability to recognize assumptions in presentations, strategies, plans, and ideas is a key element in critical thinking.
- *Evaluating Arguments:* Arguments are assertions that are intended to persuade someone to believe or act in a certain way. Evaluating arguments is the ability to analyze such assertions objectively and accurately. Analyzing arguments helps in determining a confirmation bias, that is, the tendency to look for and agree with information that confirms prior beliefs. Emotion plays a key role in evaluating arguments because high emotion clouds objectivity.
- *Drawing Conclusions:* This involves arriving at conclusions that logically follow from the available evidence. It involves evaluating all relevant information before drawing a conclusion, judging the plausibility of different conclusions, selecting the most appropriate conclusion, and avoiding overgeneralizing beyond the evidence.

Decision Making

The second outer-core competency is *decision making* (Exhibit 2.5), and it is one of the most important tasks that leaders of all levels execute. This becomes particularly challenging when a leader has incomplete or contradictory information, when the time is short, and when the impact of the decision is high. Possessing the ability to make wise decisions quickly in the context of the organization's culture is a crucial skill. The following seven elements of optimal decision making detail the specific behaviors that define great decision making:

1. *Using Your Head to Make Rational Decisions:* Collecting, analyzing, and utilizing accurate data from multiple relevant sources and objectively assessing the impact of the alternative decisions.
2. *Using Your Heart by Listening to Yourself and Others:* Making decisions that will have wide acceptance and that are aligned with the core values of the organization.

EXHIBIT 2.5:   **DECISION MAKING**

3. *Using Your Gut by Trusting Your Instincts:* Having a trustworthy gut that instinctively knows the right course of action and being able to effectively remove obstacles that might impede its implementation.

4. *Making Wise Decisions by Integrating Your Head, Heart, and Gut:* Having clear access to your head, heart, and gut so that the decision made will stand the test of scrutiny and time.

5. *Understanding the Organizational Culture:* Knowing, respecting, and—in most cases—honoring the organization's expectations regarding how decisions are best made and executed.

6. *Honoring the Organization's Decision-Making Authority Structure:* Fully understanding and utilizing the decision-making lines of authority as well as delegating decision making when appropriate and effective.

7. *Factoring in the Context of the Decision:* Effectively balancing the situation's many factors—for example, time urgency, risk level, and strategic priorities—into the final decision.

Strategic Thinking

The third outer-core competency is *strategic thinking* (Exhibit 2.6). Leaders at all levels need to fully understand the business of the organization and be able to think and act strategically on an ongoing basis. Organizational environments change rapidly, talented employees have many options for where and how they work, and customers have many choices for where to obtain products and services. When you excel in the 11 competency elements of knowing the

EXHIBIT 2.6:   **STRATEGIC THINKING**

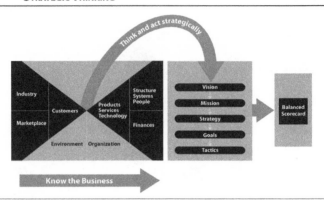

business, you enable your organization to reach the highest levels of performance, effectiveness, and efficiency. This competency contains 11 elements:

Know the Business: The Business Environment (Three Elements)

1. *Knowing the Industry:* Knowing the key environmental factors, industry trends, and being professionally networked
2. *Knowing the Marketplace:* Knowing the market, the competition,
   and your organization's strengths and weaknesses
3. *Knowing the Customers:* Knowing the needs and expectations within
   customer segments and classes and effectively responding to current
   and future customer requirements

Know the Business: The Organization (Three Elements)

1. *Knowing the Structure, Systems, and People:* Fully understanding
   how all aspects of the organization work and fit together, being able
   to successfully navigate through its systems, and designing an effective organizational infrastructure to support the work
2. *Knowing the Products, Services, and Technologies:* Maintaining a current and future view of what the organization offers its customers
   and the technology that supports this, and making deliberate and
   wise changes to these as needed
3. *Knowing the Finances:* Understanding and using a variety of financial tools as management tools and using organizational resources
   effectively and efficiently

Think and Act Strategically (Five Elements)

1. *Creating a Compelling Vision:* Developing a values-based, inspiring, and realistic vision that engages others to use it as a guidepost
2. *Defining a Viable Mission:* Clarifying the business you are in based on your unit's or organization's vision, strengths, limitations, and the desires of your present and future customer base
3. *Developing Synergistic Strategies:* Crafting a set of strategies that are integrated, that are leveraged off one another, and that enable those who work for you to achieve the mission and make effective decisions
4. *Creating Quantifiable Goals:* Setting realistic and quantifiable goals that allow people to stretch their capabilities and achieve the strategies
5. *Designing Successful Tactics:* Designing actions and activities for accomplishing each goal, utilizing these activities to achieve more than one goal when possible, and developing effective plans for their implementation

Emotional Intelligence/Leadership

The fourth outer-core competency is *emotional intelligence* (Exhibit 2.7), and it is comprised of a combination of mostly inner-core elements. These elements contribute to, or detract from, your ability to manage and monitor your own emotions, gauge the emotional state of others, and influence others. Each element has its own set of attributes:

- *Self-awareness* is the ability to recognize a feeling as it happens, to be introspective, and to exhibit strong self-confidence. It is the keystone of emotional intelligence.

EXHIBIT 2.7: **EMOTIONAL INTELLIGENCE/LEADERSHIP**

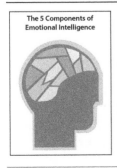

The 5 Components of Emotional Intelligence

1. **Self-Awareness**
   The ability to recognize and understand your moods, emotions, and drives, as well as their effect on others
2. **Self-Regulation**
   The ability to control or redirect disruptive impulses and moods
3. **Motivation**
   A passion to work for reasons that go beyond money or status
4. **Empathy**
   The ability to understand the emotional makeup of other people
5. **Social Skill**
   Proficiency in managing relationships and building networks

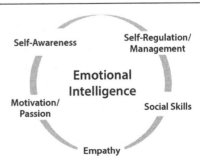

- *Self-management or self-regulation* is the ability to keep disruptive emotions and impulses in check (self-control), maintain standards of honesty and integrity (trustworthiness), take responsibility for one's performance (conscientiousness), handle change (adaptability), and be comfortable with novel ideas and approaches (innovation).
- *Motivation* is the emotional tendency guiding or facilitating the attainment of goals. It consists of achievement drive (meeting a standard of excellence), commitment (alignment of goals with the group or organization), initiative (acting on opportunities), and optimism (persistence reaching goals despite setbacks).
- *Empathy* is the understanding of others by being aware of their needs, perspectives, feelings, and concerns, sensing the developmental needs of others.
- *Social skills* are fundamental to emotional intelligence. They include the ability to induce desirable responses in others by using effective diplomacy to persuade (influence), to listen openly and send convincing messages (communicate), to inspire and guide groups and individuals (leadership), to nurture instrumental relationships (building bonds), to work with others toward a shared goal (collaboration, cooperation), and to create group synergy in pursuing collective goals. Of all the elements that comprise your emotional intelligence, this element is most readily observed by others.

Communication Skills

The fifth outer-core competency is *communication skills* (Exhibit 2.8). Being an excellent communicator is an important skill for employees at all organizational levels. For leaders, it is an essential skill. Leaders must communicate constantly in person, via telephone, in writing, and through electronic media. Leaders must also communicate effectively with a variety of people: employees at all levels, customers, vendors, suppliers, bosses, and, depending on their role, representatives of regulatory agencies, politicians, and members of the media.

- *Creating Genuine Relationships:* Being warm, open, and approachable; treating others with respect; and being regarded as a person of integrity
- *Communicating Clearly:* Communicating accurate information in a clear and timely way, using constructive formal and informal channels to do so

EXHIBIT 2.8:   **COMMUNICATION SKILLS**

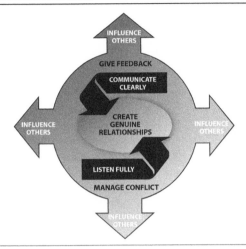

- *Listening Fully:* Giving your full attention to others when they are communicating and accurately processing what is said with a minimum of personal bias
- *Giving Effective Feedback:* Providing honest, clear, and respectful feedback to others in the organization and voluntarily soliciting feedback yourself and being open to what is said
- *Managing Conflict Constructively:* Responding to conflict, both when you are directly involved and when you are not, with a problem-solving, nonblaming approach that produces successful outcomes
- *Influencing Others:* Being able to effectively and constructively influence others in a nonmanipulative way

Talent Leadership

The sixth outer-core competency is *talent leadership* (Exhibit 2.9). In today's tough economy, leaders at all levels are facing enormous challenges when it comes to effective talent leadership. All leaders are being asked to do more with less. All leaders are worried that their top talent will be lured away by the competition as the economy improves. And all leaders are being asked to attract, select, onboard, engage, motivate, and retain employees. More than ever, accountability for executing superior talent management practices resides with leaders, not with human resources.

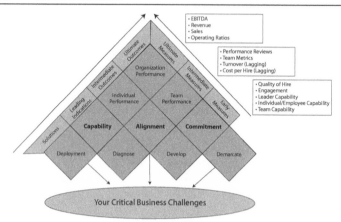

And, to be successful, leaders must understand and embrace their roles as talent leaders, in executing the four D's of talent leadership:

- *Deployment:* How to select and onboard talent
- *Diagnosis:* How to monitor individual and team engagement levels
- *Development:* How to build winning relationships, how to build a cohesive team, and how to coach
- *Demarcation:* How to give feedback, how to reward individual and team performance

Team Leadership

Team leadership is the seventh outer-core competency (Exhibit 2.10). Teams are the foundation of all contemporary organizations: work teams, cross-functional teams, matrix teams, task forces, management teams, and others. Executive leaders must master team leadership. All teams must have one or more common goals for team members and some degree of interdependence between and among members for achieving these goals. To be high performing, a team must have more than common goals and the necessary degree of interdependence required by the work itself. They need to have leadership, a vision, the right talent, an appropriate architecture or structure, effective processes, and a team-oriented culture—all to create quality products and services. Without this last element, teams may think they are high performing, but, in essence, they are performing only for themselves. Providing quality customer products and services must always be the highest priority.

EXHIBIT 2.10:   **TEAM LEADERSHIP**

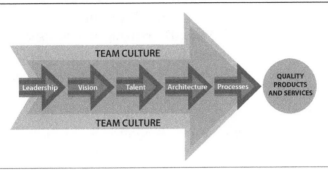

Here are the goals you should strive for when leading a team:

- *Providing Team Leadership:* Showing versatility in your leadership style, at the same time providing a consistent sense of direction for the team and using your power and authority justly and wisely
- *Creating a Team Vision:* Developing a collaborative and inspiring team-based vision that is aligned with the mission, strategy goals, and tactics
- *Attracting and Developing Team Talent:* Being the place where talented employees want to work and stay
- *Designing a Team Architecture:* Structuring all aspects of the work, from the organizational structure to the actual workflow, so that employees can do their best work without confusion or unnecessary obstacles
- *Building a Team Culture:* Creating by word and action a culture where individuals feel valued, their strengths are leveraged, and team members support one another's development
- *Assuring Quality Products and Services:* Making sure that everyone keeps the customer at the forefront, including establishing excellent relationships with vendors and suppliers

To accomplish the highest level of results in organization and teams, you need to pay attention not only to the end result, but also to six other areas along the way. When you pay close attention to these six areas, you get excellent results and get them repeatedly.

- *Setting Overall Direction and Establishing Common Goals:* Aligning

work with vision and strategy, while having effective goals, performance standards, and resource allocation

- *Creating Workable Plans:* Developing clear, realistic plans; making
  timely decisions; defining deliverables; and being flexible
- *Assigning Tasks Effectively:* Delegating to the right people with the
  appropriate skill sets in an equitable way, as well as empowering
  others
- *Expecting, Measuring, and Rewarding High Performance:* Creating
  ongoing accountability, development opportunities, and feedback;
  aligning the reward system with performance expectations; and
  modeling exemplary performance
- *Providing Ongoing Stewardship:* Knowing and monitoring the entire
  work process and the human interactions, without micromanaging,
  to address issues effectively when they arise
- *Evaluating Results and Utilizing What You Learn from the Evaluation:*
  Evaluating end results using multiple measures and doing rigorous
  post hoc debriefings, to integrate this information into future work

Change Leadership

Change leadership is the eighth outer-core competency (Exhibit 2.11). Turbulence and change have become a way of life in organizations. Being able to
manage change, at least to some degree, is something most leaders can do.
However, to take charge of change requires more mastery.

Part 1: Design the Change. To understand how to do this first requires an understanding of how to manage the three major activities involved with change:

1. *Designing* what the future of the change should look like.
2. *Assessing* the current situation in relation to the desired change.
3. *Planning and managing* the transition from the current situation to
   the desired future.

Fifteen or more years ago, most so-called change leaders first assessed
the current situation, then designed the future. Often, however, this strategy
created only small improvements because it was based on what-is and did
not take into account the desired future state. Today, change leaders first design the future in general terms, defining what they want to see in the future,

EXHIBIT 2.11:   **CHANGE LEADERSHIP**

then go back and assess the current situation. Then they design the future in more specific terms. A thoughtful and thought-through transition is critical; otherwise, there's no roadmap for moving from the present to the future. In addition, ongoing, everyday business must be managed and led at the same time as the change. This can put a great deal of pressure on leaders to execute the required change and manage business as well.

Part 2: Develop a Change Strategy. Here, the change strategy formula is very helpful:

$$D \times V \times P > R = C$$

D = demand and desire for change and the dissatisfaction with the current situation. A high D provides the motivation for the change.

V = the vision for the change, stated in a clear, compelling way that is well and widely communicated. Without a strong V, there is neither a shared direction nor a belief that those in charge of the change know where it's going.

P = the plan and process for reaching the change. This is similar to transition, but it also includes concrete information about what the organization will look like after the change occurs. Thus, P has some elements in it from design the future.

R = resistance to the change. Almost every change effort incurs resistance. With too much R, either the change effort will never materialize, or the change will occur but implementation will be very difficult. With no obvious resistance, a leader should begin to wonder why. Where is the resistance? Are we really doing something different enough?

> *C* = the change you want to occur. Although it may sound like the designed
> future already mentioned, the *C* is really more about the main goals of the
> change effort rather than the details of the design.

The change strategy formula says this: For change to occur, there must be sufficient *D* (demand, desire, dissatisfaction), sufficient *V* (a clear and compelling vision for the change), sufficient *P* (plan and process for how to get to the end results) and that all three (*D*, *V*, and *P*) must be greater than *R* (resistance to the change for the change to occur). These are the elements of the change that leaders must lead. Notice that there is a multiplication sign between the first three elements (*D*, *V*, and *P*) rather than an addition sign. This is because, if any of these elements is 0 (zero), no change will occur, even if the other two elements are strong.

Part 3: Take Charge of Change. To take charge of change while still leading and managing the ongoing business, you must take the first two areas—designing the change and developing a change strategy—and add one more element. Leaders must learn how to be a Change Champion. In Exhibit 2.10, notice that Design the Future includes anchoring or institutionalizing the change and addressing resistance. Resistance also emerges when the current situation is being assessed and people are just learning about the need for change. This is the time to increase the desire and demand for the change. Resistance will also emerge during the transition period. Leaders need to anticipate and respond effectively to the inevitable resistance that occurs during these three periods. The following six elements of taking charge of change provide more detail:

1. *Understanding the Current Situation:* Being able to accurately assess the need for change and build support for it
2. *Creating the Change Vision:* Using multiple and effective means to develop and communicate the change vision
3. *Managing the Transition:* Developing and implementing an appropriately rigorous change plan and process
4. *Reducing Resistance to Change:* Accurately identifying and effectively responding to the resistance
5. *Designing the Future of the Change and Anchoring the Change:* Constructing a well-designed change that becomes integrated into the daily life of the organization

attended to, developed, cultivated, shaped, rounded, and unleashed. So often, as I work with organizations and leaders, I find too much time and focus being placed on weaknesses and development needs instead of strengths. If you bench a perennial 300 batter in Major League Baseball, like an Albert Pujols, for one week, and you tell him he can neither hit in a game nor practice his hitting, I will guarantee that, when placed back in the lineup, he will perform poorly for a few days until he builds his repetitions back up. Leadership skills, like hitting, are very fine skills that can be enhanced only through positive repetition.

In Appendix D, when you read about building your Individual Development Plan, you will learn how to identify your indisputable leadership strengths and surprise strengths—your gifts as a leader that you must continue to strengthen. As a leader, you must also focus on identifying, in partnership with your external stakeholders, those unique development needs—indisputable and surprise development needs that will also need to be addressed. You will learn how to do this as well.

The most effective way for you to change how you view yourself and what you are capable of becoming is by changing your reference reservoir. This means learning to succeed. The more successes you can create—the more times you are able to step into that Volkswagen and drive it successfully—the more chances you will have to interpret your success as permanent, pervasive, and personal. The key to successfully internalizing these critical connections is tied to how often and how effectively you create more positively charged references. As you continue to create such references, you are faced with no choice but to interpret both the causes and consequences of those references (which are positive) in permanent, pervasive, and personal terms. At the same time, as you continue adding experiences and references to help you build a stronger, more powerful reference reservoir, you also, by definition, begin to correctly interpret whatever inevitable setbacks and failures you experience as less permanent, pervasive, and personal. All leaders must have the courage to take reasonable risks, make positive choices, accept the consequences of their behavior, course-correct, course-correct again, and never give up in their pursuit of positive constructive change for themselves and their organizations.

Achieving this is certainly easier said than done. However, a great place to start is with a positive, self-affirming value system and the development of a strong inner core. Notice in the Wheel of Intelligent Leadership™ (Exhibit 3.1) that your self-concept is truly multifaceted and complex. It consists of many

EXHIBIT 3.1:   **JOHN MATTONE'S WHEEL OF INTELLIGENT LEADERSHIP™**

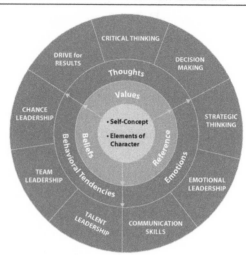

elements, including what was just discussed: your reference reservoir and belief system. But it also includes your value system, within which I always see your elements of character play out. Once you have isolated your value system, you have also isolated your character; these two facets are intertwined and cannot be separated. In Mark Rutland's, book, *Character Matters*, he defines character:

> The word *character* is from a Latin root that means "engraved." A life, like a block of granite carved upon with care or hacked at with reckless disregard, will in the end be either a masterpiece or marred rubble. Character, the composite of values and virtues etched in that living stone, will define its true worth. No cosmetic enhancement and no decorative drapery can make useless stone into enduring art. Only character can do that.

THE SIX ELEMENTS OF CHARACTER

Character has six elements:

1. Courage
2. Loyalty
3. Diligence
4. Modesty
5. Honesty
6. Gratitude

Courage

True courage—noble courage, the authentic, spontaneous act of self-sacrificial concern for the defenseless—is not fanaticism but character. Courage is not the feeling of fearlessness. It is rather the willingness of mind necessary to act out of conviction rather than feeling. Many leaders feel quite fearless but act sometimes in a cowardly manner. Conversely, I have worked with many leaders who are fearful yet behave with incredible courage. Great leaders are courageous. Courage goes beyond valor. In fact, heroism and courage are not synonymous because everyday acts of heroism are acts of impulse rather than true character. The measure of true character is consistency. We all know business heroes, public heroes, or sports heroes who were bold enough to make a heroic mark but who could not sustain their heroism over time. They misstep or fall prey to controversy, financial ruin, and criminal activity. These people were never truly courageous; they were brave at only one point in time.

Courage is the greatest character element any leader must possess because, in the face of crisis, it is the catalytic agent that mobilizes every other virtue. Knowing right from wrong is one thing; taking the right action based on this knowledge is another. Courageous leaders inspire their people and teams to innovate and achieve incredible new heights. Courage is the foundation for creating the will-do and must-do in people and teams.

Loyalty

Where has all the loyalty gone? Loyalty is the very fabric of community. Relationships cannot be developed, nurtured, or made to prosper when there is no trust to glue mutuality of commitment. When loyalty is lost, the fabric of relationship unravels. Loyalty is the willingness—because of relationship commitments—to deflect praise, admiration, and success onto others. Loyalty is a two-way street; it must function both upwardly and downwardly. In organizations, upward loyalty is shown to your boss. Are you willing to allow your boss to take credit while sometimes taking the blame? If a midlevel executive shows any disloyalty—either upward or downward—the fabric of community in that organization will begin to erode. Executive leaders must promote loyalty from the top down in order for it to become distinctly integrated in corporate culture.

Diligence

Sometimes executives are faced with challenges and may be looking for the quickest, shortest way—the easiest way—to produce the greatest returns. No such ways exist. There are no shortcuts to achieving anything worthwhile. There are countless stories of CEOs, senior executives, and entrepreneurs who are quick to reinforce this undeniable notion that there is no substitute for hard work. It is crucial for emerging leaders to connect with industry veterans who are willing to share the breadth of their experiences honestly and in vivid detail. By building these connections, the inexperienced leader may vicariously experience both the positive and negatively charged references, as well as a dose of reality and perspective. Diligence is a necessary—but not sufficient—condition for achieving leadership excellence. Diligence provides leaders with a solid foundation that will minimize the depth of their setbacks. Diligent leaders are steady performers, and steady performers are *finishers*. However, great leaders must also strive for accountability and approach their obligations with the highest degree of sincerity. Unfortunately, many managers are spiraling down toward lower maturity because of their unwillingness to finish, their reluctance to be held accountable, and their inability to follow through on their obligations. Diligence and accountability, together, work harmoniously to provide the continuous feedback loop that is necessary for individual and organizational successes.

Modesty

Modesty means living within limits. It is the opposite of being bold, that is, putting oneself forward with the sense of aggressiveness or presumption. It is the opposite of arrogance. The greatest leaders are confident. But they recognize that they are also not too good, too big, too rich, or too powerful to be open to the views and perspectives of others, especially when the information they are receiving is aimed at self- or organizational improvement initiatives. Modest leaders see fiscal and operational constraints as safeguards, not hindrances. Modest leaders are able to invoke their own limits because they realize, again through positively charged references, that greater individual and team results will be realized. Modesty is also a key counterbalancing mechanism that keeps a leader's emotions grounded. Many leaders need to know how to accept and adopt a more modest, prudent view of themselves and of the operations they run. The key to getting these leaders to transform is helping them to see that their own need for attention is driving their arrogance and the results they are achieving. If these leaders adopt a calmer, self-accepting approach in handling challenges, they will have improved outcomes and be more effective as team leaders within their organizations.

Honesty

There is a line between shrewd business and dishonesty, but that line is not nearly as fine as we think. Great leaders work hard to bend over backward for honesty because they realize truth and honesty are the pillars on which relationships, teamwork, and positive energy are built. Great leaders are comfortable missing out on deals rather than using deception to win. Great leaders would rather make a minor profit with honesty than a major one without it. Exaggerations, padded expense accounts, deliberately shaved tax forms submitted without hesitation, showing up for work late, leaving early, and theft of company property (which now reaches into the billions annually) are all acts of dishonesty. Mature leaders live and promote a truthful, aboveboard, honest existence and endeavor to replicate these ideals through the organizational environment.

Gratitude

Great leaders demonstrate enormous respect and appreciation for the sum of all their references (both positive and negative) because they know in their minds and hearts that the very essence of who they are is inextricably tied to the sum of their experiences. They know and respect that they have learned to grow and mature as leaders through their highs and lows, and they appreciate their *reference reservoirs* as nothing more than a ratio of positively charged references divided by all of their experiences. It's a batting average. Just like a batting average, the higher the ratio is, the better, but much can be learned by striking out every now and then. In fact, a strikeout keeps us in balance, and we appreciate the hits all that much more with a healthy dose of setbacks. This is one of the great challenges I see with younger executives who desire way too much, too fast; many are just unwilling to see the value in experiencing setbacks. A setback slows them down but also teaches contrast; it teaches gratitude for all experiences and special gratitude for the hits.

Gratitude, as an element of character, is also at the root of providing praise and recognition to others. Saying "Thank you" or "I appreciate you and your hard work" originates from this element; it requires selflessness but showing honest gratitude to your people and your team will propel them to new heights. Leaders who demonstrate gratitude are more personally grounded and are often better able to connect with and build relationships with team members.

CHARACTER AND VALUES

Visualize an iceberg. Beneath the water's surface is the larger volume of ice, which constitutes your character (Exhibit 3.2). Above the water's surface, the smaller volume of ice represents your *values*. Your character is always evidenced through your values, and, as a leader, you must consciously appreciate the interplay between character and values. To value something is to place importance on it, to show genuine *interest* in it. If you value money, for example, you are interested in money. You tend to read about money, talk about money, look for ways to earn money, save it, spend it, and invest it. And what you display interest in you have a favorable *attitude* toward. This attitude moves you to *act* in ways that move you toward the pleasures you have learned to associate with your values. Because you value some things more than others, you are therefore more motivated to seek the pleasures associated with some values more than others.

There are two types of values: ultimate and immediate. Ask yourself, "What do I value most?" You might answer, "Love, security, independence." These are ultimate values because they represent what you ultimately desire. On the other hand, if you answered, "I want money and family," these are more immediate values, and you need to probe further: "What will money do for me?" or "What's the importance of family in your life?"

EXHIBIT 3.2:   **YOUR CHARACTER AND YOUR VALUES**

Values

⬇

Interests

⬇

Attitude

⬇

Acts

To achieve greater levels of maturity and success, you must, as a leader:

1. Recognize the difference between immediate and ultimate values.
2. Understand your own hierarchy of values.
3. Understand where your own hierarchy of values may deviate from or align with the elements of character.
4. Set goals for sustaining your strengths and improving development needs that are aligned with only ultimate values that support the elements of character.

This is no easy task; however, the journey you take to strengthen your inner core can be one of the most rewarding ones of your life because it will show you the signs for unlocking and unleashing your massive potential. It is the path to better understanding yourself and others. It is the foundation for teaching and empowering others to become continuously more capable, committed, and connected. You just have to commit to taking that journey.

In examining your values, you need to distinguish between immediate and ultimate values. A quick way to differentiate is by asking, "Is this all there is?" If you are asking this question, it is likely that you are not connecting your goals with the pursuit of your ultimate values. Here is a list of ultimate values that are measured by the Hogan Motives, Values, and Interest Survey:

- *Aesthetics:* Art, literature, culture, imagination
- *Affiliation:* Social interactions
- *Altruism:* Desire to serve others, to improve everything
- *Commercial:* Earning money, realizing profits
- *Hedonism:* Desire for fun, excitement, variety
- *Power:* Desire for achievement, competition, getting ahead
- *Recognition:* Desire to be known, visible, self-display, famous
- *Scientific:* Analytical, new ideas, technology
- *Security:* Structure, predictability, prudence
- *Tradition:* Appropriate social behavior, morality, high standards

All 10 of these values evoke pleasure in some way, shape, or form. It is imperative that you ask yourself, "Which ones do I value more?" "Which ones do I value less?" Rank these values in order of importance from 1 to 10, with 1 being the most valued and 10 the least. You need to recognize that this hierarchy controls every decision you make as a leader and ultimately will determine the degree of pleasure or pain you experience as a result of the decisions you make.

Your values and character always play out through your personality traits and leadership style. We will see these connections directly in forthcoming chapters as we explore the Leadership Maturity Map™ and Mattone Leadership Enneagram Inventory. For example, some leaders possess a predominant Helper trait. If this is you, you tend to predominantly value affiliation, security, and altruism, as opposed to leaders who possess a predominant Driver trait and who tend to predominantly value things such as power, recognition, and commerce. Are leaders who possess different predominant traits truly different leaders? Of course they are! They possess different values, beliefs, emotions, behaviors, and skills, and they probably have different automobiles.

Although your value system will propel you in concrete directions that you tend to associate with pleasure, in fact, your past experiences (i.e., reference reservoirs) have taught you which values are the most pleasurable. Leaders who possess a predominant Driver trait, for example, have learned from their references that taking risks, taking control, and being independent have historically yielded pleasure. Because these values are associated with receiving pleasure, they have helped shape every decision they have made. These values will continue to shape whom they establish relationships with and how those relationships will develop. It also causes them to be uncomfortable in situations where they are unable to pursue the pleasure their values possess. Put a leader with an immature predominant Driver trait in a situation where they are unable to Drive, and the results are not good!

HARNESSING THE POWER OF CHARACTER AND VALUES

Once you, as a leader or emerging leader, isolate your individual values, you can now better understand why you act and behave as you do. When you start exploring your own unique value hierarchy and assess the degree to which that hierarchy either supports or deviates from the elements of character, you make it easier to see why you sometimes make a bad decision, can't make a decision, or even why your decision sometimes creates conflict. Consider this: If your number one value is security and your second value is power, you have conflicting values so close in rank that you are very likely to experience a lot of stress when making any decision.

When you do make a decision, you measure and weigh the relative probabilities that the decision will deliver either pleasure or pain. For example, suppose I ask you to go into a batting cage and try to hit baseballs thrown to you at 90 miles per hour. If the number one state that you are trying to avoid was fear, you probably would not go into the cage. But if your fear of rejection is stronger and you thought others would criticize you for not going into the cage, you would likely be more motivated to go in and face 90-mile-per-hour fastballs.

In other words, in addition to your values driving you to act in particular ways, the pleasure-to-pain ratio that you perceive and associate with experiences is also at work. Whatever pain you associate with getting into the batting cage, or with making a tough decision, or with implementing a new risky change immediately creates a variety of complex emotional states that can be counterproductive (i.e., avoiding making the decision, abdicating responsibility, etc.). However, if the perceived pleasure you associate with the same action is stronger and more powerful than the pain, you will be motivated to take action.

But which decision is correct? Clearly, if you possess a strong inner and outer core, you increase the probability that you will make the right decision. That said, however, here are some examples of emotional states that leaders try to avoid:

- Fear
- Anxiety
- Guilt
- Worry
- Sadness
- Anger
- Depression
- Loneliness

All of these states are associated with pain, but which ones are the most painful? Leaders must honestly self-reflect and rank these eight states in order of those they most want to avoid in order to learn more about how they make decisions. Assign a 1 for the states you most want to avoid and an 8 for those you find more tolerable. It is very powerful when leaders admit that the number one state they most want to avoid, for example, is fear and they then make the connection to why they are avoiding certain uncomfortable people and situations.

For you to achieve greater levels of leadership maturity as a result of continually strengthening both your inner and outer cores, you must also set development goals and create specific, targeted strategies for strengthening your unique strengths and gifts, as well as strategies for improving those develop-ment needs that are aligned with the ultimate values supporting the elements of character. You must also recognize how the values to which you assign either high or low priorities are not the result of intelligent choices as much as the result of experiences, references, and values that have conditioned you within a clearly defined complex network of pain and pleasure.

In the remaining chapters, I will introduce the Leadership Maturity Map and Enneagram in much greater detail. By using these powerful tools, you will be able to recognize your own personal leadership styles, as well as pinpoint the degree of maturity/immaturity you exhibit within your predominant trait and the traits defining your unique leadership fingerprint. As you read and think about these tools, you will also gain tremendous insight into others—your manager, peers, employees, and other important stakeholders—and learn new strategies for working with and empowering them. Clearly, as you strengthen your insights into others and develop powerful strategies for connecting with and empowering others, you will become infinitely more effective, influential, powerful, and successful.

THE VALUES PROFILE AND ELEMENTS OF CHARACTER

You determine the extent to which your values hierarchy supports or in fact deviates from the elements of character. The following is a list of ultimate val-ues along with their associated ideal priority level to which you should strive:

- Altruistic (very high priority)
- Aesthetics (low to medium priority)
- Affiliation (high priority)
- Commercial (medium priority)
- Hedonism (medium priority)
- Power (medium priority)
- Recognition (medium priority)
- Scientific (low to medium priority)
- Security (medium priority)
- Tradition (medium to high priority)

Ultimately, you must establish goals that clearly leverage your strengths (i.e., behaviors and skills that must be sustained in support of ultimate values that dem-onstrate character) and address your development needs (i.e., changing behaviors and skills to better support ultimate values that demonstrate character). To make true breakthrough changes that endure, you must:

1. Visualize in vivid detail new positively charged references that result from the positive execution of new behaviors/skills.
2. Associate (and really connect) the new positively charged references, as seen in your mind's eye, with generating a stronger pleasure-to-pain ratio than the pleasure-to-pain ratio you currently associate with the positively charged references resulting from your past or present behavior/skills. (*Note:* Feedback from external stakeholders may be helpful.)
3. Use only positive thinking and a sense of optimism.
4. Take action, sometimes little steps first, where you can generate momentum and start to associate pleasure with those little steps.
5. Remove obstacles and impediments to your achieving progress.
6. Work with key stakeholders, such as your manager, peers, and employees, showing humility and an uncompromising desire to improve by asking for their help, support, and ongoing feedback as you make the changes you need to make.

As you move through these steps, remember that real, lasting positive change is based on positive behavioral change but that, as explained, the process begins by your looking within yourself and making a commitment to strengthening your inner core. If you work hard every day—passionately and diligently taking the necessary steps to build a strong self-concept, character, belief system, references, values—your strengthened inner core will drive positive thoughts (e.g., "I can," "I will," "I must," "I am worthy of success," etc.). In turn, your positive thoughts will drive positive emotions, such as happiness, anticipation, excitement, exhilaration, and empowerment—the emotions that activate and incite positive action.

You cannot experience any emotion without first experiencing a thought. In your brain, the cognitive element *always* precedes the emotional element. For example, suppose you were at work, one of your children got sick at school, but, for some reason, nobody could get that message to you. Would you experience the emotion associated with your child getting sick? Of course you wouldn't, because you were unaware that your child was sick! The event never creates stress, conflict, or concern; only the thought about the event does that.

So, if you want to change your emotions, clearly you must first change your thoughts. In turn, positive emotions, because they incite and activate, drive positive behavior, such as constructive problem solving, relationship building, and the like, and, of course, positive behavior drives the execution of the skills and competencies that define the outer core of leadership success.

As discussed, mature leaders are positive thinkers. Immature leaders tend to be negative. Mature leaders believe in their ability to work through the challenges presented by the people and situations in their lives. This confidence would never be possible, however, without the experiences that support the validity of their thoughts. Mature leaders, then, are passionate about creating powerful success references for themselves, their employees, their teams, and their organizations. Mature leaders understand the power of references and experiences in fueling individual and collective beliefs about achieving break-through performance. Mature leaders, such as Jeff Bezos and Ann Mulcahy, recognize the powerful combination of continually renewed thought and action and how that combination propels leaders and their teams into an increasingly more mature cycle in which there is no choice but to use positive thoughts and emotions to reignite the cycle again and again.

But what about immature leaders? What about their language? As you might expect, their negatively charged references lead to negative beliefs, which lead to nonsupportive values, which lead to negative thoughts:

- I'm a failure.
- I'm being treated poorly.
- I'm a victim.
- Everyone is controlling my destiny.
- The world owes me.
- I can't do it.

All of these thoughts are either true or false depending on the leader's reference reservoir. Regardless of whether they are true or false, leaders who live with these thoughts are severely limiting their performance and potential. Leaders simply should not indulge in negative thinking. Here are three skills you can implement, in the moment, to deter negative thoughts.

Stress Inoculation

Worrying about future events creates anxiety in the present, and stress inoculation is one way to reduce that anxiety and minimize negative thinking. Imagine that a stressful performance review is coming up. Let's say that in the past, prior to previous reviews, you became worried and upset. Your boss is tough—a fast talker, insensitive, and a poor listener. A technique you can use to manage this situation is to write a message to yourself in advance of the stressful situation. Here's an example:

> Relax. Review your strengths and development needs and attempt to predict what your boss is likely to say. Be aware of discrepancies between what your manager says and what you think. Be prepared to bring these subjects up without emotion. It is possible to disagree agreeably. Rehearse your responses to anticipated feedback. Recognize that you need feedback to grow and that you are no less of a leader for accepting guidance. To discourage feedback is to diminish your right to choose how you want to behave and to lose control that comes with behaving in ways that in fact could be better.

Once you have written the message, read it aloud several times before the actual review happens, without actually memorizing it. The goal of this exercise is to get you to remember and internalize the essence of the written message so you can repeat portions of it at different times during the review without sounding rehearsed. This is a powerful skill-building exercise for executives who want to become more grounded, more knowledgeable, and more persuasive in their interactions.

Thought Stopping

Another great skill-building technique to stop the experience of recurring negative thoughts is simply to close your eyes and tell yourself, "*Stop!*" It is incredible how effective this technique is in quieting destructive thoughts. Next, you must replace the one negative thought with a positive one. The unwanted thought will probably return periodically, but if you repeat the procedure, you will increase the time it takes for that negative thought to get back into your head. Here are examples of positive self-affirming statements you can use to minimize the influence of negative thoughts:

- I am good.
- I am confident.
- I am competent.
- I am worthy of success.

- I am a gifted leader.
- I am respected.
- I am admired.
- I am a kind and sensitive leader.
- I am a major contributor.
- I can handle tough situations and people.
- I can handle anger.
- I can deal with stress.
- I will be the best I can be.

As mentioned, positive thoughts alone cannot propel you to new levels of maturity and success. You must also work hard to turn these thoughts into beliefs by creating positively charged references to support the validity of those thoughts. As slow and frustrating as this is for many leaders, it is important to repeat, rehearse, and memorize the preceding list of self-affirming statements. You, the leader, must also visualize the positive end results associated with your positive thoughts as well as the concrete steps you plan to execute in order to achieve them. Leaders must visualize in vivid detail both the steps they will take and the results they will (not hope to) achieve, describing the who, what, when, where, why, and how of the experience. By exercising this skill, you will begin to make a direct emotional connection to the positive thought; even a vicarious emotional experience such as this is often enough to stimulate positive action.

Non-Negative Thinking

Simply put, mature leaders are better than immature people at disputing the validity of their negative thoughts. One way you can practice this skill is to require proof to test the validity of your negative thought. Ask for evidence. When mature leaders hear, "I never do anything right," their immediate counterthought is, "Is that really true?" or "What exactly am I not good at?" These counterquestions help the leader dispute the validity of whatever negative thoughts they are experiencing.

Another way to dispute the validity of negative thoughts is by exploring alternative explanations. The important point is that very little happens to anyone that can be traced to one cause; most positively and negatively charged references have multiple, complex causes. You must self-reflect and analyze this complexity to acknowledge and accept that there are, in fact, multiple causes to the setbacks. Immature leaders often latch onto one cause, and usually it's the most dire.

A healthy belief system, strong character, supportive values, and positive thoughts all contribute to the development of mature emotions. Mature leaders are fully aware that they control their own emotions; they simply make the decision to be happy, passionate, and hopeful in their work and life. As explained, mature leaders are very good at mentally mapping out the positive emotions that empower them to act in mature ways. For example, if you want to improve your team player skills, you could talk about (and write down) any and all past situations where, because you were not a great team player, negative results were achieved either individually or within the organization. Perhaps you were concerned about overcontrolling the team, or you didn't want to come across as domineering. Whatever the reason, the point of this exercise is to get you to see the connection: ineffective thoughts = ineffective emotions = ineffective behavior = ineffective results.

Skill-Building Steps to Engage Positive Thinking

- Visualize the details of the situation (i.e., the who, what, when, where, why, and how), as well as the negative results—as painful as this might be.
- Verbalize what you have just visualized.
- Ask yourself follow-up questions, such as, "What did you do to handle the situation?" or, "By submitting to others, did that solve the problem?"
- Verbalize your current feelings and emotions based on the details of what you have expressed.
- Now, work with yourself to internally commit to change.

Once you have mapped out a failure scenario, you need to visualize a situation—even if you have few references to support it—where being a better team player will lead to feelings of excitement, exhilaration, and success. First, visualize offering ideas to the team, solving problems with the team, opening up and listening to alternative views, and enjoying the success that comes with both leading and participating with your team. You must visualize again in vivid detail, as you did in the failure scenario. Again, verbalize what you have visualized; use follow-up questions to envision and verbalize successful steps being executed and great results being achieved. The point of this exercise is to strengthen your brain's cognitive associations between acting on your developmental goal of improving your team player skills and success, both individual success and collective success for your organization.

THE POWER OF VERSATILITY

In this age of accelerating change and complexity, mature leaders must demonstrate versatility. Versatility is independent of predominant leadership type, although some types, as we will learn when we explore the enneagram, have a stronger predisposition to being versatile. Versatility is the most important of all behavioral tendencies because it also represents a measure of social endorsement. Leaders who have learned how to meet the demands of others in a wide variety of situations will, more often than not, receive support and endorsement from those they have helped. On the other hand, those who have been less resourceful in meeting the varied needs of others will often receive less support and endorsement. To be versatile is to observe and empathize. Great leaders are able to recognize others' needs and empathize with their emotions. As a result, these great leaders enjoy stronger, more vibrant relationships and higher levels of maturity and success. Versatility is the bridge that connects a leader's inner-core attributes to their outer-core tactical skills and strategic competencies.

Here are some starting points for building your versatility skills:

- Be pleasant; smile more.
- Remember names.
- Ask questions about others' interests.
- Listen.
- Support what you hear.

You will notice that these behaviors are basic in concept but amazingly difficult to apply consistently. The theme of great leaders, though, is, "What can I do to make it easier for others to relate to me?" One place to look for an initial answer to this question is in areas of commonality. Versatile leaders search their experiences for whatever ideas or events they might have in common with people they wish to relate to. The more you can find to share, the greater probability will be of effective communication. To the extent that leaders and their bosses, peers, employees, or any others for that matter share more interests, they achieve greater levels of communication. Ironically, the levels of nonverbal communication increase with the rising number of shared interests. Gestures come to take the place of words. And that is how it should be. Nonverbal communication is the simplest, purest form of communication and is often less likely to be misunderstood because it emerges straight from feelings. Uncluttered, uncomplicated, and uncontaminated by thought, nonverbal communication represents the true self.

To reach this level of communication, versatile leaders know that the initial encounters with others necessitate modifying their style and self-monitoring without being phony. What makes this skill so difficult to master—for all leaders—is the inner tension that's created when they temporarily abandon their own comfortable style to assume one more fitting to the individual or situation. Fortunately, whatever modifications leaders make are temporary. When commonality is achieved, you are able now to gradually return to the ways with which you are most comfortable.

The alternative to style modification is to refuse to make any effort to adjust—to label as wrong or inferior what often is merely different. Labeling is a common practice of immature leaders and is designed to help them avoid the tension associated with having to make changes; it saves them work. Leaders who modify their style begin with a decision to accept others' styles as legitimate and authentic as their own. The next step is to stretch your style to include the qualities common to those to whom you want to relate better. To be truly versatile, then, is to give more to others than might be expected of you. True versatility and maturity know no limits and are not tied to personality types.

CHAPTER

4

Map of Leadership Maturity™—The Enneagram

Traditionally, power has been concentrated at the top of organizations. However, unrelenting external and internal challenges—fierce global competition, an aging baby boomer population, instability in the financial and job markets, and increased corporate governance—have forced organizations to rethink how they identify, promote, and develop leaders. Organizations have also responded by creating flatter structures and transferred decision-making authority to employees throughout the organization. In essence, organizations now require individuals at all levels to be leaders; to thrive and survive in today's organization, all employees must be leaders.

Unfortunately, not all employees are ready and willing to take on the leadership responsibilities their organizations want (and need) them to have.

An examination of how society is structured reveals why. From the moment of birth, people have held subordinate roles in society. At birth, people are exposed to their first bosses, their parents. Children accepted the leadership of their parents because they were entirely dependent on them. As a result, most children are used to being told what to do by their parents. Seldom do children tell their parents what to do. Once children entered school, they were exposed to other bosses, their teachers. Similarly, if they attend church, mosque, or temple, they were exposed to a similar power dynamic in the form of priests, ministers, rabbis, or mufti. Thus, by the time they enter an organization that grants them the power to make decisions, many individuals may have no prior leadership or decision-making experience to draw on.

Without the necessary skill or experience in leadership, most young leaders will default to leading based on their own values and beliefs—their inner core. Unfortunately, most young leaders are not entirely aware of their own values, beliefs, strengths, or weaknesses; ultimately, the combination of these elements serves to shape and define a leader's unique style.

The Map of Leadership Maturity™ is a powerful tool that will help you, the leader or emerging leader, gain the necessary self-understanding required to recognize your own strengths and development needs. Secure in the knowledge of who you are and what your potential is, you will now be poised to execute better decisions, lead change, build teams, communicate, and resolve conflict in ways that will propel you to higher levels of success, yielding massive payoffs for the employees, your teams, your organization, and yourself. As a leader who approaches and executes every day with a renewed self-awareness, you will now be able to read and understand other people and successfully build a strong and stable bridge of versatility that connects your inner core with your outer-core competencies and skills.

The Map of Leadership Maturity™ (Enneagram) distinguishes among nine distinct leadership traits (Exhibit 4.1). Although everyone exhibits an inner core and behavioral tendencies primarily associated with one predominant trait, everyone also demonstrates, to a lesser degree, an inner core and behaviors associated with the other traits. The exact origins of the enneagram remain unknown. Some trace its origins to Babylon in 2500 BCE. Many agree that the Sufis popularized the use of the enneagram in the tenth century. The word itself comes from the Greek words *ennea*, meaning "nine" and *gram*, meaning "something written or drawn." Each of the nine points on the enneagram

EXHIBIT 4.1: **THE ENNEAGRAM**

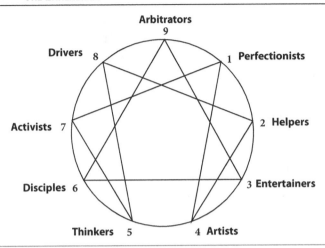

corresponds to a distinct way of thinking, feeling, and behaving. Thus, people at different points on the enneagram view the world and interact with it differently. The enneagram continues to be used after thousands of years because of one simple reason: It works.

The enneagram offers notable advantages over other psychological assessments. The main advantage of the enneagram is that it identifies the strengths relative to the maturity level associated with a leader's inner core attributes— thoughts, feelings, values, beliefs, and behavioral tendencies. The enneagram correlates with other well-known personality and behavioral assessments that are based on the five-factor theory (e.g., Myers-Briggs, DISC, and Hogan); however, the enneagram provides more granular detail regarding leadership maturity and further defines clear development paths so that leaders can more accurately define and target their development goals and strategies.

Many other approaches to leadership development focus primarily on changing behaviors and may result in only short-term changes. Without understanding why they act the way they do, leaders may fall back to their original behavioral patterns after a while. Falling back on old habits is more likely to occur in stressful and uncertain situations, the very types of situations that characterize most workplace environments today. Thus, interventions that focus solely on behavioral change are likely doomed to fail. Only by understanding the underlying reasons for your actions can lasting change occur.

The enneagram identifies the underlying factors that you, the leader, value most. Once you understand your deep-seated values, you will have a stronger appreciation for why you act the way you do. This, in turn, can cause you to make lasting behavioral change. The enneagram also offers greater precision than other psychological assessments. Instead of categorizing people into four or five broad categories, the enneagram recognizes that, although every leader has a predominant trait, they also possess the other eight traits to a varying and lesser degree. In fact, I have discovered that leadership success is less a function of the traits that predominate in any one leader and more a function of the relative maturity with which the traits are exhibited.

After many years of using the enneagram in my coaching, when I see leaders and future leaders who evidence higher levels of maturity—all things being equal—they tend to enjoy higher rates of promotion, career success, and life balance. The Map of Leadership Maturity™ is the only known enneagram that specifically addresses current and emerging leader development, growth, and maturity. My original book on the subject, *Success Yourself* (MasterMedia, 1996), was the first book ever written applying the enneagram to leader development and business. Since then, as a result of coaching hundreds of leaders all across the world and my ongoing research, I continue to refine my ideas and teachings on the subject. I would like to now share with you the best of what I have learned.

BREAKING DOWN THE MAP OF LEADERSHIP MATURITY™ (ENNEAGRAM)

The Map of Leadership Maturity™ consists of a circle divided into three main parts, or groupings:

- Heart Leaders
- Head Leaders
- Gut Leaders

Note that the Map does not pigeonhole people as possessing traits related to only one of the groupings. It recognizes that everyone is guided by Heart, Head, and Gut. At the same time, different people tend to exhibit characteristics presented in one of the groupings more than the other two. In other words, everyone has a tendency to predominantly rely on a Heart, Head, or Gut leadership style, just as everyone has a tendency to predominantly rely on one of the traits more than the others. That said, as you read about the triads and traits in the forthcoming sections of the book, when I refer to someone as a perfectionist, for example, I am referring to the fact that the predominant leadership trait is perfectionist, and therefore the person should not be labeled as a perfectionist leader. You will see that your leadership style and how you present your style to others is multifaceted, complex, and well beyond simply attaching one overarching label as a means to describing you and how others see you.

But each of these groupings is too broad to accurately capture the variety and complexity of leadership behavior. For this reason, each of the three major groupings is subdivided into three distinct personality subtypes:

- *Heart Leaders* tend to be Helpers, Entertainers, or Artists.
- *Head Leaders* tend to be Activists, Disciples, or Thinkers.
- *Gut Leaders* tend to be Drivers, Arbitrators, or Perfectionists.

Similarly to how people tend to be more Feelers, Doers, or Relaters, people tend to exhibit behavioral characteristics associated with one subgroup more than the others. In other words, someone who is predominantly a Feeler may be predominantly a Helper, Entertainer, or Artist. At this point, understanding the differences among the nine subcategories is not important. Those differences will become clearer in subsequent chapters and through use of the Map of Leadership Maturity™.

In other versions of the enneagram, which do exist, you might notice that the names (e.g., Helper) attached to numbers of the enneagram vary. For example, in other versions of the enneagram, you might see the name Loyalist attached to the 6, whereas in our enneagram the name Disciple is attached to the 6. Nevertheless, the numbers remain constant regardless of the names used. This is why some people refer to themselves in terms of their number rather than their name. Whatever the names used, The Map is the only known enneagram that specifically addresses current and emerging leader development, growth, and maturity.

Each of the subcategories within the three overarching categories differs in its relationship with the dominant trait in the overarching category. One of the subcategories will overdevelop the character trait, another will underdevelop it, and the last will be out of touch with it. For example,:

- In the Heart Leader Triad, Helpers have overdeveloped their feeling characteristics, Entertainers are out of touch with them, and Artists have underdeveloped them.

- In the Head Leader Triad, Activists have overdeveloped their thinking characteristics, Disciples are out of touch with them, and Thinkers have underdeveloped them.
- In the Gut Leader Triad, Drivers have overdeveloped their Gut characteristics, Arbitrators are out of touch with them, and Perfectionists have underdeveloped them.

Each of the nine subcategories will now be discussed in greater detail.

Heart Leaders

Regardless of whether someone is predominantly a Helper, Entertainer, or Artist, Feelers share characteristics relating to how they feel about themselves and others (Exhibit 4.2). Their greatest strengths and greatest weaknesses are their emotions. When these leader types develop in mature ways, their feelings are the focus of what is admirable about them. Conversely, their feelings are the source of most of their problems. Derailing Heart Leaders perceive that they cannot be respected and appreciated for their own sake. As a result, they develop a broad spectrum of strategies to earn the respect and appreciation of others. The central problem facing derailing Heart Leaders typically involves their identity. Instead of developing their true identities, they will sometimes focus their energies on developing socially admirable identities. Helpers (Twos) focus on making themselves likeable to others. Entertainers (Threes) direct their energies to building a respected/successful social image. And Artists (Fours) try to differentiate themselves from others, seeking uniqueness and individuality. When Helpers, Entertainers, and Artists are frustrated in their attempts to identify and communicate their feelings, they often resort to hostility toward others or, in the case of many Artists, toward themselves in the form of being overly critical of themselves.

- *Mature Twos (Helpers)* are admired and appreciated for their ability to sustain positive and mature feelings for others. Because of their overdeveloped feeling characteristics, Helpers are able to understand people and empathize with them well. Mature Helpers tend to be kind and generous, and they go out of their way to help others without expecting anything in return. Average Helpers are generous, but, unlike mature twos, they use their generosity to control the behavior of those they've been generous to. Derailing Helpers see themselves

EXHIBIT 4.2:   **HEART LEADERS**

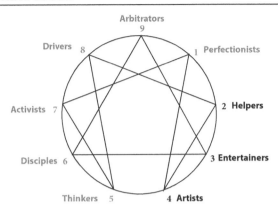

Heart Leaders (Twos, Threes, Fours): All have challenges relating to their feelings or, to be specific, with their image. Twos can be intrusive and overly emotional, and they often overexpress their feelings. Threes, who can ignore their feelings in order to get the job done and be successful, are the most out of touch with their feelings. Fours, despite feeling emotions deeply, usually don't like to express them directly and instead communicate usually through subtle communication or an art form. They therefore underexpress their feelings.

---

as loving and generous, but they're selfish and manipulative. *Note:* No Helper is exclusively unselfish, controlling, or manipulative, just predominantly so. Although healthy Helpers can exhibit the behaviors of a derailing Helper, that isn't likely.

- *Mature Threes (Entertainers)* are valued because of the social services they perform. Entertainers adapt themselves well to others and gain admiration for their ability to do so. However, Entertainers may project an image substitute for who they really are because they are out of touch with their feelings. Average Entertainers are driven to project a socially valued image to gain admiration and respect. Although derailing Entertainers are similar to average Entertainers in that they project a socially valued image, they differ from average Entertainers in their application of energy toward getting even with those who do not appreciate them.

- *Mature Fours (Artists)* are intuitively self-aware. They are able to communicate their most personal feelings and are liked because of their ability to help others get in touch with their feelings. Average

Artists are in touch with their feelings but tend to focus predominantly on negative emotions. As a result, average Artists tend to become withdrawn and prefer their own imagination over what they can share with others. Derailing fours become so negative about how they feel about themselves that they become self-hating. Average and derailing Artists can be considered to have underdeveloped feeling characteristics because of their tendency to dwell on negative emotions.

Head Leaders

Thinkers (Fives), Disciples (Sixes), and Activists (Sevens) share characteristics relating to their ability to think and get things done (Exhibit 4.3). Mature Head Leaders are known for their outstanding achievements; less mature Head Leaders range from those who can't complete tasks, to those whose accomplishments are counterproductive, to those whose behaviors are completely out of control. Whereas the central problem facing less mature feelers relates to their identity, the central problem facing Head Leaders relates to their insecurities. The search for safety and security can lead Head Leaders to withdraw into an intellectual world they can control (Thinkers), or to follow the will of an authoritative figure or institution (Disciples), or to constantly engage in some form of activity (Activists).

- *Mature Fives (Thinkers)* are capable of turning their brilliant thoughts into actions and are valued for their ability to solve problems. At their core, Thinkers are analyzers. Average Thinkers also have great ideas, but they're so concerned with making sure their ideas are correct that they rarely act on them. In other words, average Thinkers are paralyzed by analysis. Derailing Fives think so much that they become isolated as a result of their thinking and may have a hard time distinguishing what is real from what is not. Thus, average and derailing Thinkers can be considered to have overdeveloped thinking characteristics because of their inability to turn their thoughts into action.
- *Mature Sixes (Disciples)* are loyal, committed, and almost always dependable. Average Disciples are also loyal and committed, but they are unable to act unless they secure some form of permission from either a person in authority or an authoritative belief system. Average

EXHIBIT 4.3:   **HEAD LEADERS**

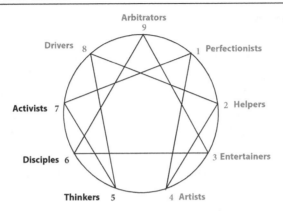

Head Leaders (Fives, Sixes, Sevens): All have challenges with their thoughts and sometimes fear and anxiety. Fives tend to think and think again and again, live in their minds, and often overexpress their thoughts. Sixes can often trust others more than themselves and are the most out of touch with their thoughts. Sevens often avoid introspection and turn to the outside world for action and experience, making them underexpress their thoughts.

Disciples may also sometimes act rebelliously in order to prove to themselves that they are independent of the authority they identify with. Derailing Disciples are so dependent on authority that it leads to feelings of inferiority. Their self-hating and self-destructive tendencies often result in rejection from the authority they identify with. In essence, Disciples may be out of touch with their sense of thinking because they are unable to act on their own.

- *Mature Sevens (Activists)* accomplish many things in many fields. Activists are very busy people, and each day is not long enough to accomplish their goals. Average Activists are also very busy and accomplish goals, but they are satisfied with only a few of them. Unhealthy Activists busily spin their wheels in a frenzy of hyperactivity but accomplish very little because they lack focus and direction. By constantly keeping busy, derailing Sevens hope to avoid having to deal with their insecurities. In essence, Activists face the problem of having underdeveloped thinking characteristics.

Gut Leaders

Drivers (Eights), Arbitrators (Nines), and Perfectionists (Ones) are concerned with how they relate to their environments (Exhibit 4.4). Eights want to dominate it, Nines want to coexist with it, and Ones want to perfect it. The central problem that Gut Leaders face is their frustration with an imperfect world. Drivers can become frustrated with their lack of standing in the world, Arbitrators become frustrated when people fail to live up to the idealized image they hold of others, and Perfectionists become frustrated with what they perceive as the deficiencies of others and their environments.

- *Mature Eights (Drivers)* are confident and able to inspire confidence in others. This ability enables Drivers to accomplish a lot and help others reach levels of accomplishments that they could not reach alone. The tendency for Drivers to see themselves as better than everyone else leads them to have an overdeveloped sense of relatedness. Average Drivers are still able to achieve a lot, but, rather than leading and inspiring others, they step all over them on their way to the top. This tendency to exploit others often sabotages the ability of average Drivers to reach the top because their avenging enemies put a stop to

Exhibit 4.4:   **Gut Leaders**

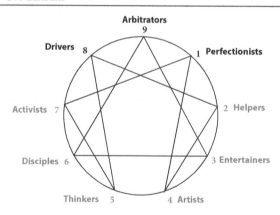

Gut Leaders (Eights, Nines, Ones): All have challenges with anger and relating to others. Eights are assertive and hardworking, and they tend to overexpress their anger. Nines are friendly and laid-back, and they can be the most out of touch with their anger. Ones have perfectionist tendencies, often suppress emotions, and can underexpress their anger.

them. Derailing Drivers are fixated on reaching the top; they exploit others to even a greater degree than average Drivers, again sabotaging their likelihood of actually achieving their objective. They tend to excel at creating enemies.

- *Mature Nines (Arbitrators)* are able to sympathize and empathize with others. Through their ability to accept and understand, they make people feel comfortable and assured. Average Arbitrators understand themselves and others, but they have a tendency to idealize people they relate to. By placing other people on pedestals, average Arbitrators create an image that people can't possibly live up to. When people fail to live up to their idealized image, Arbitrators can feel a profound sense of disappointment. Derailing Arbitrators hold onto their false and idealized illusions to the point that they often alienate themselves from reality. In essence, average and derailing Arbitrators are out of touch with their relatedness with others. Instead of seeing people for who they are, these Arbitrators see them as symbols.

- *Mature Ones (Perfectionists)* are able to influence people through their clear understanding of issues and their innate ability to distinguish right from wrong. Perfectionists tend to be reasonable, logical, and fair. Average perfectionists attempt to be objective and rational but allow their emotions to cloud their judgment. This leads average Perfectionists to try to force their environments into their view of absolute perfection. Because everything in their lives can be improved, even excellence is not satisfying. Derailing Perfectionists are so obsessed with the deficiencies of others and their environments that they fail to see their own weaknesses and shortcomings. Average and derailing Perfectionists both face problems with their underdeveloped ability to relate to others. By constantly trying to perfect those around them, Perfectionists have difficulty accepting people for who they are.

How to Use the Map of Leadership Maturity™

Having read these very brief descriptions of the nine leadership traits that make up The Map, you may be able to place yourself or others you work with in one of the triads (Feeling, Doing, or Relating), but perhaps not into a predominant trait. One way to help you isolate your predominant trait is to ask other people with whom you work. Of course, to accurately identify your predominant leadership trait, as well as the degree of maturity with which you exhibit the thoughts, attitudes, values, and behaviors of your predominant trait and each of the other eight traits, you can take the Mattone Leadership Enneagram Inventory (Appendix C). As suggested in Chapter 1, nobody will stop you from completing the MLEI right now, but I believe you will gain much more by first reading this book and reflecting on all you have learned before actually completing the MLEI.

One of the goals of The Map is to make you aware of the changes you need to make in order to become an outstanding, mature leader. To succeed, you must be willing to address the unpleasant truths about yourself, eliminate your current limiting thoughts and behaviors that are preventing you from becoming the leader you are capable of becoming, and *passionately* and *diligently* work hard to accept and implement the critical changes that you will need to make in order to unleash your massive leadership potential. By actively addressing the challenges associated with your own predominant trait and learning about the other traits, I know you will grow and mature as an individual leader. I am confident your hard work will strengthen your *capability* as a leader. As discussed in Chapter 1, only under the umbrella of your ever developing capability can you create the magical environment in which your people and teams become more capable, committed, and connected. Are you ready for the challenge? Let's go!

One of the major advantages of The Map is that it details the paths for increasing maturity for each of the nine traits. To reach increasing levels of maturity, The Map lays out the following paths of development:

$$1 \rightarrow 7 \rightarrow 5 \rightarrow 8 \rightarrow 2 \rightarrow 4 \rightarrow 1$$

or

$$3 \rightarrow 6 \rightarrow 9 \rightarrow 3$$

In other words:
- Someone who is predominantly a mature, predominant One (Perfectionist) should logically work to acquire and develop the behaviors of a mature, predominant Seven (the Activist).
- Likewise, a mature, predominant Seven (Activist) should work to

acquire and develop the behaviors of a mature, predominant Five (Thinker).

- Mature, predominant Threes (Entertainer) should work to acquire and develop the behaviors of a mature, predominant Six (the Disciple).
- And so on.

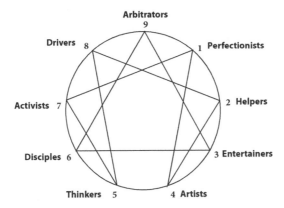

Conversely, The Map's next representation indicates its negative directions:

$$1 \rightarrow 4 \rightarrow 2 \rightarrow 8 \rightarrow 5 \rightarrow 7 \rightarrow 1$$

and

$$3 \rightarrow 9 \rightarrow 6 \rightarrow 3$$

In this sequence:

- Derailing, predominant Ones (Perfectionist) should learn to recognize and avoid the derailing behaviors of a predominant Four (Artist).
- Likewise, a derailing, predominant Four (Artist) should learn to recognize and avoid the derailing behaviors of a predominant Two (Helper).
- And so on.

The Map goes beyond the static characterization of traditional personality assessments by showing the dynamic nature of leadership traits. For example, suppose a predominant Four successfully avoids adopting the behaviors of a derailing, predominant Two and further manages to successfully acquire and develop the behaviors of a mature, predominant One. The Four does not stop growing and developing as a leader at One. Rather, after mastering the positive attitudes, thoughts, emotions, and behaviors of a mature, predominant One, the Four should continue to take on challenges by working to acquire and develop the behaviors of a mature, predominant Seven.

The Map also shows that leaders can move toward increasing immaturity. For example, a derailing, predominant Six (Disciple) runs the risk of acquiring the derailing behaviors of a derailing, predominant Three (Entertainer). Whereas the derailing, predominant Six leader will experience extreme anxiety and may be suspicious, the derailing, predominant Six who is now taking on the characteristics of a derailing, predominant Three will strike out at those perceived to be threatening.

Your goal in using The Map is to accurately identify your predominant leadership trait and then work passionately and diligently every day to acquire, develop, and cultivate the mature characteristics of that trait. Once you have developed and cultivated the mature characteristics of your predominant trait, you can move on to acquiring and developing the mature characteristics of all the traits that define the essence of great leadership.

CHAPTER

5

Understanding Your Helper Leadership Trait

Leaders who are predominant Helpers have strong feelings for others. Ironically, this very positive attribute can also be the source of many of the challenges they encounter. Helper leaders can tend to overexpress their positive feelings toward others and dismiss their negative feelings in their attempt to deal with the challenges they face at work. Their sense of self is that they are sensitive, caring leaders, yet, when they are derailing, their acts of kindness and care are not free; they want something in return. At some point, Helpers who derail come to believe they should get back in respect and kindness what they gave out. This is why leaders who demonstrate the derailing side of the Helper type often come across as needing to "buy" respect and admiration; they will see to it that others admire and respect them. Not only are they effective in getting others to accept that they have no choice but to show them admiration and respect, but also that they are also very good at making others feel guilty if they don't reciprocate. Derailing Helpers are also unaware of the pressure they can put on others. There always seems to be a silent expectation; they are always looking for more attention, a bigger response.

Mature Helpers, on the other hand, are considerate and genuinely the most sensitive and caring of all the leadership types. Because they have strong feelings toward others, they will go out of their way to help their employees, their team, their boss, their clients—everyone. They are passionate about selflessly serving others. As they derail, however, Helper leaders can become dishonest about the presence of their aggressive feelings; consequently, they rarely see themselves the same way others see them, namely, as manipulative. Derailing Helpers respect and admire others but always with strings attached. Even though they have strong needs for inclusion and affection, they are careful not to overexpress this need.

At their inner core, leaders who possess a predominant Helper trait can have a problem with their identity. Derailing Helpers often deny their aggressiveness toward others and frequently conceal their hostility even from themselves. In fact, the only time they act aggressively is when they have convinced themselves they are behaving this way only for someone else's benefit. To admit their aggressiveness contradicts their self-image and potentially alienates the people they may need later. Derailing Helpers therefore deny their selfish or aggressive motives or interpret them as appropriate. As they perfect this mode of leadership behavior, the distance between the Helpers' motives and behaviors becomes significant. The result is that they tend to force others into situations in which the Helper controls everything, which can cause those who are being controlled to become frustrated because of the control and the sense of being obligated to show the Helper gratitude. The major focus of derailing Helpers, then, is on themselves, although they never want to think they are giving this impression to others or think of themselves this way.

Recognizing the Mature Helper Trait in You
- Prefer close relationships.
- Support and actively listen to others.
- Are warm, accepting, and friendly.
- Work slowly and cohesively with others.

- Tend to be agreeable, steady, calm, and supportive.
- Share personal feelings.
- Demonstrate effective coaching skills.
- Handle conflict effectively.
- Encourage support from others.
- Prefer to be on a first-name basis.
- Are more relationship-oriented than task-oriented.
- Are generous, unselfish, and show respect and care for others without strings,

Recognizing the Middle-of-the-Road Mature Helper in You
- Tend to talk more about your own feelings than those of others.
- Talk more about care, respect, and admiration than truly executing these traits.
- Are emotionally demonstrative.
- Give attention to others to the point of flattery.
- Can be solicitous to the point of meddling.
- Interfere a lot under the guise of caring.
- Try to control those you have "invested" in.
- Want people to depend on you.
- Want to be informed about everything.
- Like to be sought out for advice.
- Expect to be constantly thanked and honored for the good you bring.

Recognizing the Derailing Helper in You
- Complain a lot and are often resentful.
- Disguise your motives behind friendly gestures.
- Are manipulative and self-serving.
- Try to make people feel guilty.
- Undermine others by disparaging them.
- Control others to the point of being domineering.
- Feel entitled to get what you want.
- Are disappointed when favors are not repaid.
- Feel victimized and used.
- Rationalize your responses to others' ingratitude.

If you are a mature, predominant Helper, in order to move toward increasing levels of leadership maturity, you need to follow the sequence presented on The Map as: 2 → 4 → 1 → 7 → 5 → 8. In other words, one of your objectives is to create a specific, compelling development path that enables you to start to acquire and cultivate the mature attributes of the Four (Artist). If this is you—a mature, predominant Helper—you have already accepted the presence of your negative feelings as completely as you have accepted your positive feelings. Because you have learned to become emotionally honest, you are now able to express your full range of your emotions. As a result, you do not play the conditional respect game; you have learned to accept others unconditionally. Respect and admiration are given to you because of who you are, not what you have done for others.

Derailing, predominant Helpers, on the other hand, when they are not spiraling toward greater maturity, run the risk of acquiring even more immature characteristics, starting with the derailing traits of the Eight (Driver). Your negative progression on The Map runs like this: 2 → 8 → 5 → 7 → 1 → 4. The major issue with derailing, predominant Helpers is that they have not come to grips with their aggressive feelings. They resent those who are ungrateful to them and are quick to strike out at those who have not responded to them the way they wanted.

HELPER LEADERSHIP STYLE

When you are mature, you enjoy compatible relationships with your employees, team, peers, boss, and clients. You show patience and staying power, and are motivated to make relationships work. You are generally uncomfortable with conflict unless you are moving toward greater maturity. You are vigilant about how others complete tasks but will rarely say anything negative about what you observe; this is typically seen with middle-of-the-road maturity in Helpers. When you are mature, you are a great coach and teacher because of your selflessness in your need to help others. You seek inclusion and desire to work with people on a first-name basis. You tend to seek more in-depth friendships at work than the other leadership types. You are also a great listener and expect others to listen as well. You are open and expressive about your thoughts and feelings, and likewise you expect the same from others.

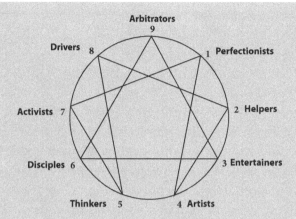

When *Helper* leaders talk to themselves, here's what they say:

Basic Fear
I fear being disrespected and being shown no gratitude for what I have done for others. I fear that others will not respect or admire me unless I make others respect and admire me.

Basic Motivation
I have a strong need to be admired and respected.

My Greatest Irritation
I work hard to respect and care for others. I don't understand why they would not respect and care for me in return.

The Spark That Ignites My Defensiveness
I think that all my actions are done with good intent, that I connect with others without condition, and that there are no other ulterior motives that define my relationships with others.

My Greatest Potential Weakness
I am involved in goodness that calls attention to itself so that my goodness will be admired. I want to be seen as good, humble, and self-sacrificing and want my generosity repaid.

My Greatest Potential Strength
I can be a giving person. I can admire and respect others unconditionally. I do not need thank-you's. I help others for the sake of others.

TIPS FOR STRENGTHENING THE HELPER TRAIT IN YOU

- Ask yourself what your manager, employees, and key stakeholders need and help them attain it. Giving people what they need and not necessarily what they want or what you think will make them happy makes you truly helpful.
- Let your quality of service, your unselfishness, and goodness stand on their own merits. Be respectful of genuine talent and encourage real strengths. Be generous without attaching strings. If you are good, people will seek you out and respect you. You don't have to manipulate others into liking you.
- Be more conscious of your need to be liked and the sometimes conditional games you can play, as in "I like you; therefore you must like me." When you play this game, you pressure yourself and others to satisfy an agreement that exists only in your head.
- Don't call attention to yourself and your efforts. After you have helped someone, let it go. Don't look for a return.
- Don't fall into the trap of trying to get people to like you by giving undeserved praise. Conversely, don't withdraw support from those you don't like. What you do for others should not be based solely on what they have or have not done for you.
- Cultivate new relationships, but don't forget to honor your primary relationships.
- Work behind the scenes more, and don't advertise the good you do.
- Try not to be possessive or controlling. Everyone deserves to have their own experiences.
- Be sure your motives for helping others are pure and unselfish. Don't hide behind intentions you know are insincere; you will never be judged on intentions, only on your actions.

TIPS FOR WORKING WITH PREDOMINANT HELPERS

As you read this book and begin to practice the strategies for growing, maturing, and becoming more versatile, learn to separate your reactions to people from their reactions to you. If, from their behavior, you can identify people as predominant Helpers, here are some tips for strengthening your connection with them:

- Take the initiative to show you are interested in them as people. Ask about what's important to them as leaders and individuals, and then support them in terms of their stated needs. Working cohesively and collaboratively with Helpers works best.

- Mature Helpers generally want to work in concert with their manager to support the goals of the group or organization. They recognize they can increase their chances for even greater success through cooperation and collaboration. Helpers will go above and beyond for their manager and organization, and they can be a positive force when their goals are truly aligned with the goals of the department or organization.

- When setting goals with Helpers you lead, exercise patience and encourage them to open up about unstated goals. Helpers tend to verbalize spontaneously about other people's goals, not about their own personal goals. You must keep them focused on articulating their own goals so that you can be in a better position to help them achieve those goals. You may have to work closely with the Helpers you lead to learn the specifics of the who, what, when, where, why, and how of their goals.

- Be careful not to exaggerate your interest with Helpers because, if they sense that you are coming on too strong, they can become disappointed and distant.

- If you agree on a development goal and action steps and they begin to take action, make sure to check back in early to see how they are progressing. Ask whether they have any hesitancy about the validity of the goal or action steps previously agreed to. Sometimes, Helpers will agree prematurely in order to avoid a potential conflict. Use these check-ins as opportunities to role-model for your employee that airing disagreements can be done effectively up-front, in an open, honest, and professional manner. Helpers need to develop a reference reservoir so that they see that mutual respect can be given and received, even in the face of conflict.

- Helpers tend to be less disciplined about time. Be aware of this as a leader when facing hard deadlines and make sure to allocate time resources accordingly. Give Helpers ample time to execute their personal developmental goals. Be patient and, if at all possible, don't force them to make decisions too quickly. You will ultimately have more success if you move slowly, cautiously, casually, and informally with the Helper; patience is a key requirement.

- Show you care. If you listen and are responsive to the Helpers you lead, you will sometimes get them to share all their feelings, including the negative ones. Remember that Helpers tend to overexpress their positive feelings and underexpress their negative feelings. The Helper will generally value candidness, openness, and honesty from peer groups and supervisors.

- Be patient. Helpers use opinions as opposed to facts to avoid the risks associated with making important changes. Building rapport, along with earning trust and credibility, is key to influencing the Helpers' commitment to organizational action. Helpers sometimes will ask for a personal guarantee that the action you want them to take is the correct one; however, the action they actually take is much more the result of Helpers' own decision and commitment.

AWARENESS EXERCISE: BUILDING UP YOUR HELPER TRAIT

In the spaces provided, record your responses:

Provide a leadership example in which you exhibited immature/derailer Helper traits.

_____

_____

_____

_____

Thinking back on this situation, what were the consequences of your immature actions? What happened?

_____

_____

_____

When you acted immaturely, please describe in vivid detail the thoughts and feelings you experienced prior to taking the action you did.

_____

_____

_____

_____

Based on what you have read in this book and you reflecting on this situation, write a brief summary of how your thoughts, emotions, actions, and results were connected.

_____

_____

_____

_____

If this situation were to present itself again, what end result would you desire? Please provide vivid detail about the result, those who would most likely be impacted, and why they would be impacted. Please detail the who, what, when, where, why, and how associated with the end result you desire.

_____

_____

_____

_____

To achieve this new desired result, please indicate the actions and strategies you would take to ensure that the new desired end result would be achieved. Again, please detail the who, what, when, where, why, and how of your strategies. What stakeholders/mentors will you reach out to for their guidance, feedback, and support of your strategies?

_____

_____

_____

_____

In order to execute these actions and steps, what thoughts and emotions would need to be in place to support your positive actions?

_____

_____

_____

_____

After executing your new plan/strategy, what results were achieved, and what did you learn?

_____

_____

_____

_____

CHAPTER

6

Understanding Your
Entertainer Leadership Trait

Leaders who are predominantly Entertainers are perhaps the most driven to succeed. Believing that they will be admired and respected only if they deliver results, Entertainers become fixated with success and appearing successful. In essence, success becomes the central component of Entertainers' self-concepts. Everything else can become a secondary priority. Their singular focus on fame and recognition allows Entertainers to thrive in organizations where style is seen as more important than substance and where symbols win out over reality. An Entertainer who is in charge of an organization may try to create such an organization.

Mature, predominant Entertainers gain the respect of others because of their drive, determination, and hard work. Other people become inspired by the dedication and energy of mature Entertainers. Through their own efforts and their effects on others, mature Entertainers can accomplish tasks that were thought to be impossible. As they begin to derail, however, Entertainers direct more effort toward image building than task accomplishment. Instead of accepting who they are and focusing on working hard, derailing Entertainers focus their efforts toward appearing like winners. They study how to dress, talk, and network like winners. However, at the end of the day, derailing Entertainers have neither achieved success nor developed an authentic inner core. Given the precariousness of their image, derailing Entertainers become jealous and hostile toward anyone who challenges their success. Incapable of producing any tangible evidence of their success, derailing Entertainers may resort to hostility and manipulation to deal with those who challenge their projected image.

At their inner core, Entertainers are out of touch with their feelings. Connection with their true feelings and self is lost because their energy is directed toward building their social image. Entertainers fear that their true self is unworthy of respect and admiration, and as a result they turn to their successes and image to gain the respect and admiration of others. As Entertainers derail, the gap between their true self and projected self becomes greater. Instead of developing their inner core, derailing Entertainers become fiercely competitive for all forms of success and prestige, turning every situation into a competition. Entertainers become so focused on the outcome—winning—that they overlook how they achieve success, sometimes opening the door for unethical and illegal practices. Entertainers also have tremendous difficulty dealing with failure. Because failure directly challenges their self-image of success, Entertainers may devote enormous amounts of energy into trying to turn unsuccessful projects into successful ones. Instead of walking away from lost causes, Entertainers may pour more and more resources into a sinking ship. Immature Entertainers may also direct enormous amounts of energy toward sabotaging and attacking those who are more successful than they are. Instead of finding ways to be more successful themselves, they seek out ways to undermine the success of others. As derailing Entertainers deteriorate, they run the risk of becoming superficial, narcissistic, and completely incapable of empathizing with anyone's feelings or needs.

Recognizing the Mature Entertainer in You

- Are self-assured, confident, and charming.
- Are direct, fast-paced, and enthusiastic.
- Listen and speak well.
- Persuade and motivate people.
- Can be influential and popular.
- Adapt well to changing conditions and remain optimistic.
- Desire self-improvement.
- Know your strengths and weaknesses.
- Can be dramatic in their actions and opinions.

Recognizing the Middle-of-the-Road Mature Entertainer in You

- Are pragmatic, efficient, and goal-oriented.
- Are hypercompetitive and believe winning is the most important thing.
- Can be manipulative and calculating.
- Value style over substance.
- Constantly worry about the how other people see you and the image you project.
- Constantly compare yourself to others.
- Have an inflated sense of self, which often leads to grandiose expectations and arrogance.
- Exaggerate accomplishments to draw attention to self.

Recognizing the Derailing Entertainer in You

- Are immoral, untrustworthy, devious, and jealous.
- Are opportunistic and exploit others.
- Do not tolerate others winning.
- Undermine those who have moved ahead.
- Often stab colleagues in the back for personal gain.
- Manipulate others to achieve your ends.

If you are a mature, predominant Entertainer, in order to move toward increasing levels of leadership maturity, you need to follow the sequence presented on The Map as: 3 → 6 → 9. In other words, your objective is to create a specific, compelling path that enables you to start to acquire and develop the mature attributes of the Six (Disciple). If this is you—a mature, predominant Entertainer—you have learned that, by committing to someone other than yourself, more can be accomplished by working together than against one another. By acquiring and cultivating the mature attributes of the Disciple, you also have learned that your own self-image is not diminished in any way, shape, or form as a result of committing to others. If you are a mature, predominant Entertainer, you accept the essence of who you are and you no longer need to strive to achieve a definition or image of success that previously may have controlled you. In addition, you now recognize that feeling good about yourself, in fact, is a better definition of success. Because you feel good about yourself, you no longer feel the need to sabotage others who are successful. You now realize that the success of others does not take away from your own success. This outlook enables you, the mature, predominant Entertainer, to gain trust and commitment from others. The respect and admiration you now receive are due to who you are, not what you have achieved.

Derailing, predominant Entertainers, on the other hand, when they are not spiraling toward greater maturity, run the risk of acquiring even more immature characteristics, starting with the derailing traits of the Nine (Arbitrator). Your negative progression on The Map runs like this: 3 → 9 → 6. When derailing, predominant Entertainers begin to acquire and develop the derailing, predominant traits of the Arbitrator; they further lose touch with their feelings. Derailing, predominant Entertainers are driven by their hostility, but derailing, predominant Entertainers who possess immature Arbitrator traits lose touch of their hostility. They are left feeling nothing. Without hostility to drive them, derailing, predominant Entertainers are without zest or energy. They are no longer motivated to accomplish anything or even to project an image of success.

ENTERTAINER LEADERSHIP STYLE

When you are mature, you can win over people at all levels of an organization, whether they are subordinates, teammates, peers, bosses, or clients. You are goal directed, optimistic, and fast paced. Additionally, you are great at selling yourself and your ideas. You are also capable of leveraging ideas and innovations from everyone throughout an organization. Feeling that desks are confining, you typically move about the office, talking to nearly everyone from the custodian to the boss. You are good at getting people to open up and prefer to

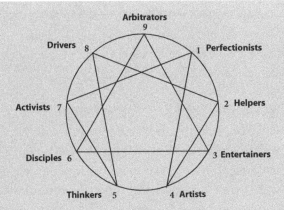

When *Entertainer* leaders talk to themselves, here's what they say:

Basic Fear
I fear being a failure. I fear that others will not respect or admire me unless I achieve great things.

Basic Motivation
I want to be the best and be on top. I want to get better, rise above my competition, and impress others.

My Greatest Irritation
I am a superior person who has worked hard to get where I am today, and people don't recognize it.

The Spark That Ignites My Defensiveness
I compare myself to others even though I know I should measure my behavior against more objective principles and values. I compete with others over everything, and I want to be the best at everything.

My Greatest Potential Weakness
I am more interested in packaging the product than the product itself.

My Greatest Potential Strength
As I mature, I will develop myself without comparison or competition. I accept my limitations.

be on a first-name basis with people. By brainstorming with everyone, you can bring out good ideas that may have never surfaced. Because you are naturally talkative and people oriented, you often seek out visible leadership positions where you can achieve popularity and recognition.

Tips for Strengthening the Entertainer Trait in You

- Develop collaborative relationships with customers, supervisors, and stakeholders. By considering the feelings and opinions of others and working with others to identify mutually beneficial outcomes, you will gain their respect and support. People are more motivated to help you succeed if they play a role in making decisions and also benefit from those decisions. In essence, by becoming more interdependent, you can achieve greater success than you could alone because teams can accomplish more than any individual.
- Tone down your competitive instincts. Recognize that you can't win all the time. Remember that no one likes the person who constantly has to one-up everyone. To curtail this instinct, focus on value-comparisons instead of other-comparisons. In other words, instead of measuring your personal and organizational success based on how you perform relative to others, focus on measuring your success based on your values (i.e., my work improved the lives of people).
- Do not self-aggrandize yourself. Don't exaggerate, brag, or inflate your importance. People respond more favorably to people who are honest about their accomplishments and share the glory. After all, why would people help you out if they know you will take all the credit?
- Guard against the Entitlement Fallacy. You are not entitled to something just because you want it. Recognize that desire and obligations are different and that others have the right to say "no" to you. You may also have to say no to others from time to time. To help cope with this tendency, remember that you are free to want, but others are free to say no.
- Develop your own identity. Many derailing, predominant Entertainers clone themselves after models they perceive to be successful. By avoiding this tendency, you can focus on developing your own strengths and correcting your weaknesses. This strategy will ultimately help you develop greater maturity and further define your

individual competitive advantage as well as the competitive advantage of your firm.

- Learn to support others by congratulating peers and subordinates for their accomplishments. By supporting them through hard times, you will gain the respect of others.
- Lower your expectations for acclaim. If people like what you are doing, they will tell you. If they don't give you superior accolades, you may be thinking of yourself in a more favorable light than is realistic.

TIPS FOR WORKING WITH PREDOMINANT ENTERTAINERS

- Ask questions about their opinions and ideas. Letting Entertainers share their vision shows them that you respect them enough to give them your time.
- Look for ideas that they find exciting, and work with them to shape their ideas into successes.
- Discussing your ideas in a stimulating, entertaining, fast-moving, storytelling manner is the best way to get the attention of Entertainers. Motivational stories about people and situations that support your ideas in a positive way are effective ways of influencing Entertainers.
- Supporting your ideas with the opinions of others is more effective than facts and details when trying to convince Entertainers. Show how other people and organizations have benefited from the actions you are asking them to take. Entertainers respond well to actions that lead to recognition.
- Be sure to work out the details of an idea. Entertainers tend not to focus on the details. Focusing on the who, what, when, where, why, and how can strengthen their ideas and increase the probability of success. If they are not interested in the details, summarize what's been discussed and make suggestions for improving the idea. You may need to pin them down on details later.
- Ask what you can do to help them come up with a plan of action for implementing their ideas.
- Don't compete or argue. Disagreements threaten Entertainers to the point that they often become fixated with winning an argument rather than finding a solution. Rather than saying "I disagree," opt

for, "Here's another alternative" or "Here's another option you might consider."

AWARENESS EXERCISE: BUILDING UP YOUR ENTERTAINER TRAIT

In the spaces provided below, please record your responses:

Provide a leadership example in which you exhibited immature/derailer Entertainer traits.

_____

_____

_____

_____

Thinking back on this situation, what were the consequences of your immature actions? What happened?

_____

_____

_____

_____

When you acted immaturely, please describe in vivid detail the thoughts and feelings you experienced prior to taking the action you did.

_____

_____

_____

_____

Based on what you have read in this book and you reflecting on this situation, write a brief summary of how your thoughts, emotions, actions, and results were connected.

_____

_____

_____

_____

If this situation were to present itself again, what end result would you desire? Please provide vivid detail about the result, those who would most likely be impacted, and why they would be impacted. Please detail the who, what, when, where, why, and how associated with the end result you desire.

_____

_____

_____

_____

To achieve this new desired result, please indicate the actions and strategies you would take to ensure that the new desired end result would be achieved. Again, detail the who, what, when, where, why, and how of your strategies. What stakeholders/mentors will you reach out to for their guidance, feedback, and support of your strategies?

_____

_____

_____

_____

To execute these actions and steps, what thoughts and emotions would need to be in place in order to support your positive actions?

_____

_____

_____

_____

After executing your new plan/strategy, what results were achieved and what did you learn?

_____

_____

_____

_____

CHAPTER

7

Understanding Your
Artist Leadership Trait

Leaders who are predominant Artists are perhaps the most creative and innovative leaders. The creativity of Artists is driven by their deep understanding of themselves. Unfortunately, this tendency to engage in deep introspection can lead to many problems. Derailing, predominant Artists often feel they lack self-worth. This, in turn, makes them uncomfortable in their social roles and relationships with others. As a result, derailing, predominant Artists may avoid carrying out their leadership responsibilities and let their employees direct themselves. Artists can become so self-involved that they lose touch with everyone but themselves. They stop paying attention to the needs of others and exist in their own world. Artists in this state can make illogical, unrealistic, and counterproductive demands of their employees, teammates, and sometimes even their own manager. Artists may not even realize how off-the-wall or unreasonable their demands are. Although Artists can produce works of beauty on their own, sometimes they have difficulty working with others to produce works of beauty. This is due to their intense self-focus. By spending so much time and energy diving into themselves, Artists have little left to devote to others. Consequently, Artists may not notice the needs of others and neglect coaching and developing people. In the end, they may resort to doing things themselves.

Mature Artists, on the other hand, possess the potential to bring out the most in people. Because they can sense in themselves the depths to which people can descend as well as the heights to which people can ascend, Artists are perhaps the most aware of the potentials and predicaments of human nature. Their ability to understand what is at the core of each person enables Artists to move people deeply. This in turn allows Artists to be effective champions of causes. As Artists become increasingly mature, they draw less inspiration from themselves and more from others. By forming meaningful and deep connections with other people, Artists become more grounded in reality and are better able to shape it into what they imagine. As Artists derail, however, they direct increasing amounts of energy toward themselves and less toward expressing how they feel to others. Instead of channeling their feelings toward building things that can move and inspire people, Artists escape into their imaginations. The more withdrawn Artists become, the more they lose touch with reality and their ability to shape it.

Like Helpers and Entertainers, Artists face problems with their identity. Artists believe that they are different from other people. This desire to understand why they are different fuels their deep introspection. If Artists cannot determine why they are different, they run the risk of self-hate. Seeing themselves as defective, they become hostile to themselves. Derailing Artists are highly self-destructive leaders. Their constant focus on themselves and their defects leads them to lose touch with other people. With their inability to focus on other people, derailing Artists often alienate other people. They allow whatever emotions they experience at the moment to surface. Although Artists believe this is a sign of their being genuine, others interpret this as a sign that they are prone to frequent mood swings. The tendency for Artists to have manic highs and debilitating lows puts their employees on edge; they never know what to expect. This instability also makes it nearly impossible to present a clear vision and direction to employees, teammates, colleagues, and clients.

Derailing Artists frequently shift their priorities. Consequently, a million projects may be undertaken, but none are completed.

Recognizing the Mature Artist in You

- Are creative and intuitive.
- Are introspective and comfortable being alone.
- Are sensitive to yourself and others.
- Respect others and show compassion.
- Accept your feelings and act authentically.
- Can and do reveal your feelings
- Can openly discuss your fears.

Recognizing the Middle-of-the-Road Mature Artist in You

- Are moody, easily hurt, and not very practical.
- Are imaginative to the point of fantasizing.
- Can be self-absorbed to the point of being shy.
- Express your emotions indirectly.
- Withdraw from conflict.
- Have difficulty expressing your feelings to others.

Recognizing the Derailing Artist in You

- Are depressed, overly negative, and angry at yourself.
- Constantly feel drained and fatigued.
- Can't discuss your ideas or feelings.
- Remain detached from people with no strong connections.
- Avoid any kind of responsibility.

If you are a mature, predominant Artist, in order to move toward increasing levels of executive maturity, you need to follow the sequence presented on The Map as: 4 → 1 → 7 → 5 → 8 → 2. In other words, one of your objectives is to create a specific, compelling development path that enables you to start to acquire and cultivate the mature attributes of the One (Perfectionist). If this is you—a mature, predominant Artist—you have learned to move out of the world of subjectivity and self-absorption and into the world of objectivity and principled action, which is characterized by mature, predominant Perfectionists. Focusing on objectivity and action will enable you to build real and tangible success. Success, in turn, will produce positive feelings and emotions and counter your tendency to experience negative emotions. As you begin acquiring and developing the mature, predominant traits of Perfectionists, you now begin to accept that you must submit to values and expectations. This will enable you not only to feel a sense of connection with others and decreased sense of isolation, but also enable you to remain focused on objectives. The more you, the mature, predominant Artist, acquire and cultivate the mature, predominant traits of Perfectionists, the more self-disciplined you become. By not being controlled by your emotions, you learn how to perform consistently as a leader despite the many inevitable personal ups and downs you will experience.

Derailing, predominant Artists, on the other hand, when they are not spiraling toward greater maturity, run the risk of acquiring even more immature characteristics, beginning with the derailing traits of the Two (Helpers). Your negative progression on The Map runs like this: 4 → 2 → 8 → 5 → 7 → 1. Derailing, predominant Artists have an overwhelming desire to escape themselves and their introspection. They accomplish this by becoming dependent on another person who provides them with the direction and understanding they need. The problem with this dependency is that they are no longer capable of leading others. Instead, they become the enforcer of another person's will.

ARTIST LEADERSHIP STYLE

Mature, predominant Artists are good at stimulating creativity. They are able to see how each task fits into the greater whole. As a result, Artists are good at mixing things up and altering tasks to create novel products and services. If innovation is needed, mature Artists can help stimulate it in others. Artists are also cautious and methodical leaders. They tend not to make decisions based on impulse. Instead, decisions are made after much deliberation and introspection. Artists are very good at asking themselves questions and exploring problems from multiple angles. Additionally, Artists tend to lead based on their own ideals and conviction. This offers other people a sense of stability because knowing the values of an Artist enables others to predict their likely actions. Artists, however, are not perfect leaders. Due to their deep deliberation, Artists tend to be slow decision makers. As a result, they may not be the most suited for leadership positions in time-sensitive industries or operations. Furthermore, derailing, predominant Artists fear failure more than other leadership types and can be quick to become negative when faced with setbacks.

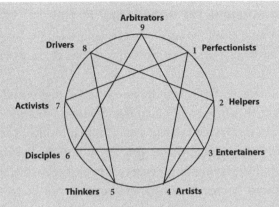

When *Artist* leaders talk to themselves, here's what they say:

Basic Fear
I fear being defective or inadequate in some way.

Basic Motivation
I want to understand who I am—my thoughts, my feelings, my unconscious—so that I can become all that I'm capable of becoming.

My Greatest Irritation
I am misunderstood by others and don't fit in.

The Spark that Ignites My Defensiveness
I often retreat to imagination and fantasy in my pursuit of self-understanding. I get so caught up in myself that I waste precious time.

My Greatest Potential Weaknesses
I'm jealous of others who seem normal and able to fit in easily.

My Greatest Strength
As I mature, I will achieve emotional balance in my life. I will no longer be vulnerable to my emotions and capable of solving problems, I'll take action, and turn negative situations into positive experiences.

Tips for Strengthening the Artist Trait in You

- Don't let yourself be controlled by your feelings. See your feelings as part of who you are but not the singular characteristic that defines you.
- Avoid negativity. By avoiding negative thoughts and instead engaging in the positive self-affirming ideologies discussed in Chapter 3, you can thwart the cycle of criticism that results in your immobility.
- Don't procrastinate. Waiting until you are in the right mood only results in inaction and causes difficulty with managing time and resources. More often than not, you will not be in the right mood to carry out a task. Furthermore, there are certain tasks on the job that people are seldom in the mood to perform. Learning to perform these tasks despite your feelings is a necessary step toward developing consistency. Accomplishing a little each day is more sustainable and more likely to result in real-world success than waiting for rare moments of inspiration and frenzied activity.
- Start small, and break tasks into incremental components. Don't try to change the world or make a work of art your first time out. True works of art and innovation rarely occur on the first endeavor. Removing the burden of making a masterpiece will allow you to experience small incremental successes, which in turn will set you up to experience greater successes later.
- Improve your self-discipline. Sleeping consistent hours, eating healthy foods, and exercising regularly can improve your mood. Your improved mood will provide you the energy you need to jump-start the projects you want or need to undertake. Also, schedule in blocks of time. This will help you focus your efforts toward the specific tasks you need to complete. By establishing a routine, you will be able to accomplish what you need to accomplish despite the feelings you are experiencing at that time. Remember, self-discipline is not an obstacle to your freedom if the discipline comes from you and is driven by your broader goals.
- Redefine failure as a unique opportunity to learn. Failure is necessary for learning and self-improvement. You don't know everything and you will make mistakes, both personally and on the job. Failure does not indicate that you are an inferior person; it merely indicates

that you need to continue to grow. By learning from your mistakes, you will become better at what you do. Viewing failure as a reflection of your underlying inadequacies will only immobilize you from taking action, solving problems, and growing as a person.

- Try not to take things personally when on the job. When your boss criticizes you, don't take it as being reflective of the whole truth about you. Criticize yourself less and focus instead on the criticism itself. The criticism may have no basis in reality. In that situation, you should just brush it aside. Alternatively, the criticism may contain valuable feedback on how to improve your performance. In that situation, you must pay attention to the criticism because it can ultimately lead to valuable personal or organizational-level improvements. If you focus only on criticizing yourself as a worthwhile person, you may miss out on valuable developmental opportunities.
- Talk openly to people whom you trust. Talking to close friends will show you that you are not as different or as much of an outsider as you think. Finding who you are and developing your unique self-concept is as much an outside search as it is an inside search.
- Focus on the present and future. Artists have a tendency to get caught up in the past. Complaining about the past and how things haven't gone your way does little to improve your present and future situation. Instead, focusing on how to fix your present and future can lead to better outcomes.

TIPS FOR WORKING WITH PREDOMINANT ARTISTS

- Build a supportive, safe work environment to connect with the Artist. Artists tend to be warm, approachable people when mature, but distant to the point of being uncommunicative when immature. For Artists who are not fully mature, take time to make them feel accepted and adequate. Don't force them to take action too quickly, or they will reject you and your ideas. Patience is the key when dealing with Artists.
- Take your time. Because Artists tend to act slowly, building a relationship with an Artist may take a while. Demonstrate that you support the Artist's feelings and ideas. Because immature Artists often have negative self-worth, they may interpret criticism of their ideas as an attack on their self-worth.

- Build their confidence. Immature Artists tend to view themselves as inadequate. Consequently, one of your primary objectives when supervising Artists is to build their confidence. You can do this in a number of ways. First, Artists can be reminded of their past individual or organizational successes. Often, Artists become so negative that they focus only on past failures. By drawing attention to successes, Artists begin to see that they can be successful despite previous failures.

- Artists can also be given small developmental exercises to help them gain focus, something as simple as brainstorm 10 possible ways of dealing with x problem. By giving Artists more focused, proximal goals, you can better direct their efforts. This will prevent Artists from trying to solve big problems out of the gate. Instead of becoming dissuaded by their inability to successfully solve large-scale problems and getting caught up with their grandiose visions from solving these problems, Artists are actually able to solve a problem when they break the problem into smaller chunks. This exercise will help build their confidence because instead of getting caught up in their imagination and inaction, Artists begin to learn the importance of breaking bigger problems into smaller ones that are more approachable and actionable.

- When working with Artists on decision making, acknowledge the importance of their intuition, but identify other factors that help as well. Because Artists tend to rely on introspection, they often base their choices on intuition. Consequently, it is important for you as a supervisor to initially support their gut feelings. Discuss times when their feelings guided them to the correct decision. Also identify the cues that likely affected their feelings. This way, Artists begin to see that their intuition is a reaction to cues in their environment. By doing this, you can help Artists to become less dependent on their feelings while helping them to learn the importance of supplementing their feelings with additional information when making decisions.

AWARENESS EXERCISE: BUILDING UP YOUR ARTIST TRAIT

In the spaces provided, please record your responses:

Provide a leadership example in which you exhibited immature/derailer Artist traits.

_____

_____

_____

_____

Thinking back on this situation, what were the consequences of your immature actions? What happened?

_____

_____

_____

_____

When you acted immaturely, please describe in vivid detail the thoughts and feelings you experienced prior to taking the action you did.

_____

_____

_____

_____

Based on what you have read in this book and reflecting on this situation, write a brief summary of how your thoughts, emotions, actions, and results were connected.

_____

_____

_____

_____

If this situation were to present itself again, what end result would you desire? Please provide vivid detail about the result, those who would most likely be impacted, and why they would be impacted. Please detail the who, what, when, where, why, and how associated with the end result you desire.

_____

_____

_____

_____

To achieve this new desired result, please indicate the actions and strategies you would take to ensure that the new desired end result would be achieved. Similarly, please detail the who, what, when, where, why, and how of your strategies. What stakeholders/mentors will you reach out to for their guidance, feedback, and support of your strategies?

_____

_____

_____

_____

To execute these actions and steps, what thoughts and emotions would need to be in place in order to support your positive actions?

_____

_____

_____

_____

After executing your new plan/strategy, what results were achieved and what did you learn?

_____

_____

_____

_____

CHAPTER
8

Understanding Your Thinker Leadership Trait

Leaders who are predominantly Thinkers like to analyze the world around them. They prefer thinking to doing and often become out of touch with the practical reality of working in an organization. Thinkers also have a hard time translating impulses into action. Many Thinkers will not act until they are certain of what they want to do. In fact, Thinkers can become so engrossed with their thoughts that they lose touch with everything else.

Mature Thinkers are capable of comprehending complex phenomena at a glance. They thoroughly analyze problems from multiple angles and ask questions that get people to challenge the basic assumptions they used in solving a problem. Not only are mature Thinkers capable of understanding problems, they are able to explain these problems to others in a comprehensible manner.

Because the perceptions of mature Thinkers are closely aligned with actual reality, their decisions tend to be sound and logical. As Thinkers begin to derail, however, they become increasingly disconnected with reality. Derailing Thinkers seek to distance themselves from others in order to clear their heads and analyze problems objectively. Unfortunately, derailing Thinkers use distance to admit only the kinds of information that confirms their mental perceptions of the world. This often leads them to become narrow-minded, rigid, and extremely conservative. As Thinkers further retreat into their intellectual world, they reduce complexity into simplicity. This tendency to simplify problems has the ironic effect of immobilizing them from taking action because they now fear of acting without planning for every contingency.

At their inner core, Thinkers have trouble dealing with their insecurities, which are often triggered by unpredictability and uncertainty in their environment. As a protective mechanism, Thinkers learn to be vigilant of their surroundings and to anticipate problems before they occur. Through understanding and explanation, Thinkers develop a sense of security. Although these tendencies can be adaptive, Thinkers tend to overdevelop them at the expense of other characteristics. For instance, Thinkers tend to be out of touch with their feelings. They tend to analyze things before they feel a response to them. Many Thinkers seek to distance themselves from their feelings because the predominant feeling they experience is fear. Fear is a guiding force in the lives of Thinkers; they fear being controlled and allowing anyone or anything to control their thoughts. Because their self-worth is based heavily on their ability to defend the validity of their ideas, Thinkers feel diminished if another person proves them wrong. To protect themselves from this fear, derailing Thinkers resist testing their ideas in the real world and keep them to themselves.

Recognizing the Mature Thinker in You

- Are independent, innovative, and visionary.
- Are cerebral, objective, and mentally alert.
- Are eager to learn and excited by discovery.
- Ask insightful questions.
- Can distinguish patterns and predict how current events will end.
- Capable of acting without complete information.
- Are willing to discard theories that are no longer relevant.
- Are unafraid of uncertainty.

Recognizing the Middle-of-the-Road Mature Thinker in You

- Are slower-paced, tentative, and methodical.
- Have relatively weak interpersonal skills and can become argumentative when others disagree.
- Retreat into your thoughts when stressed.
- Think like scientists but interpret facts according to your theories.
- Constantly dissect things intellectually but jump to conclusions.
- Focus on details to the point of losing sight of the big picture.
- Fear acting without complete knowledge.

Recognizing the Derailing Thinker in You

- Are reclusive, secretive, and self-contained.
- Are antagonistic toward those who disagree with you and prone to arguments.
- Have difficulty connecting with people.
- Become isolated from people and reality.
- Don't care about being socially acceptable.
- Distrust authority and rules.

If you are a mature, predominant Thinker, in order to move toward increasing levels of leadership maturity, you need to follow the sequence presented on The Map as: 5 → 8 → 2 → 4 → 1 → 7. In other words, one of your objectives is to create a specific, compelling path that enables you to start to acquire and cultivate the mature attributes of the Eight (Driver). If this is you—a mature, predominant Thinker—you have learned to overcome your fear of the environment, and you have learned to trust the people and situations that comprise your world. As you learn to trust people and situations, your confidence grows. You now realize that, despite not knowing everything, you still know a lot more than anyone else. You also discover that acting without complete knowledge is better than inaction. As you turn more of your thoughts into action, you learn that objectivity and certitude are illusions. You now realize that you can never be completely objective, and, therefore, you begin to trust your feelings when making decisions.

Derailing, predominant Thinkers, on the other hand, when they are not spiraling toward greater maturity, run the risk of acquiring even more immature characteristics, starting with the derailing traits of the Seven (Activist).

Your negative progression on The Map runs like this: 5 → 7 → 1 → 4 → 2 → 8. The major issue with derailing, predominant Thinkers is that their over-thinking has inhibited their taking positive action. Wanting to overcome this roadblock, derailing, predominant Thinkers begin to act first and think later. Unfortunately, their actions jump from being measured and controlled to being impulsive and erratic. Whereas previously too much thought preceded action, now too little occurs.

Thinker Leadership Style

When you are mature, you like to create structure for yourself and your employees. You like orderly, systematic approaches that enable you to understand everything. You prefer intellectual or consultative leadership roles, as opposed to authoritative or inspirational leadership roles. You tend to take your time when making decisions because of your desire to be as accurate as possible. You seek out details, specifics, and facts when making decisions. Unfortunately, however, you may never feel secure enough to act and often fail to make decisions or take action. This is typically seen in middle-of-the-road and derailing, predominant Thinkers, who possess the capability of becoming the world's busiest procrastinators.

Tips for Strengthening the Thinker Trait in You

- Analyze less and observe more. The more you analyze an environment, the greater the likelihood is that you distort it and impose preconceptions on it.
- Don't jump to conclusions. Be open to new information as it comes in, and use it to modify your existing theories.
- Seek advice from someone whose judgment you trust. Thinkers have difficulty deciding on the optimal course of action. By consulting with someone you trust, you may find it easier to make decisions.
- Try to be cooperative. Learn to yield without feeling that you have been beaten intellectually or that you have been put in a vulnerable position.
- Try to be more considerate of others. Your brilliance may intimidate others and make them feel uncomfortable. Because you are so wrapped up in your ideas and what interests you, it's easy to forget basic courtesies.

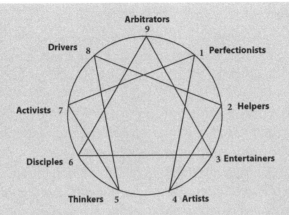

When *Thinker* leaders talk to themselves, here is what they say:

Basic Fear
I fear that someone will invalidate my view of reality.

Basic Motivation
I want to understand the world around me—to observe everything, to be certain that my views are correct, and to reject those views that are incorrect.

My Greatest Irritation
I get upset when someone questions my intelligence.

The Spark That Ignites My Defensiveness
I analyze things thoroughly because, through analysis, I can control my environment, gain insight, make predictions, and protect myself if necessary. I become so focused on details that I sometimes lose perspective.

My Greatest Potential Weakness
I am so hungry for knowledge that I sometimes forget the importance of other things.

My Greatest Potential Strength
I am capable of understanding things. I am able to comprehend many points of view at the same time and be compassionate and tolerant of different viewpoints as opposed to being cynical and detached.

- Share your ideas. You can benefit others by sharing your insights, especially when your views are critical to understanding a problem. Offering a realistic, logical suggestion that has a probability of making things better, even though it isn't perfect, is better than saying nothing at all.
- Be less critical and demanding of yourself and others. Accept the fact that reality and life are not perfect, and accept the fact that you are not perfect.
- Learn to express your emotions. Bottling your emotions behind a wall of objectivity keeps you disconnected from people. Identifying with people and showing compassion will allow you to develop relationships with others. In other words, don't use just your head; use your heart as well.
- Take time to relax. Thinkers tend to be intense and high-strung and find it difficult to relax and unwind. Taking time to calm yourself will enable you to analyze situations from a fresh perspective.

TIPS FOR WORKING WITH PREDOMINANT THINKERS

- Demonstrate your willingness to help through your actions rather than your words. Thinkers tend to focus more on tasks than on developing relationships. Consequently, demonstrating your ability to help Thinkers complete tasks will earn their trust. Saying that you are there to help but doing nothing to help will do little to earn the trust of a Thinker.
- Focus on specifics, facts, and details. Thinkers do not respond well to flashy plans with little substance. Thus, stay away from testimonials from other people, gimmicks, and personal incentives. Your ability to get accurate facts and discuss them with the Thinker in a logical, predictable way will strengthen your relationship. Focusing on the advantages and disadvantages of a plan and ways to overcome the disadvantages is an effective way of communicating with Thinkers.
- If you disagree with Thinkers, argue on the basis of fact. Be careful not to use the word *disagree*. Many Thinkers view disagreement as a direct challenge to their intelligence. Don't push too hard that you are correct and they are wrong.

- Acknowledge the Thinker's competence. Statements such as, "I respect your viewpoint because I consider you an expert" go a long way toward diffusing potentially needless conflict.
- Encourage Thinkers to consider alternative viewpoints. One way of presenting alternatives without threatening Thinkers is to frame alternatives as detours. In other words, you may wish to say, "I realize that this may not be what we end up with, but we could take a few minutes to see if there is something useful here." You can also encourage Thinkers to extend their concepts or theories over time and space by asking, "How will that concept look in practice?" or "Can you tell me how that will look in a year?" These kinds of questions move your discussion from a conceptual level to a concrete level.
- Thinkers are risk averse. To successfully influence a Thinker, provide evidence that what you say is based on substance, not someone's opinion. Thinkers want to be sure that any decision made today will be just as valid in the future. Any evidence that you can provide them that the future will not deteriorate will go a long way toward getting Thinkers to agree with you and your position.
- Take your time. Don't rush Thinkers into making up their minds before they have had ample time to review the decision for themselves.
- Agree on a schedule for the implementation of an idea. Make sure to write down the who, what, when, where, why, and how of your plan.

Awareness Exercise: Building Up Your Thinker Trait

In the spaces provided, please record your responses:

Provide a leadership example in which you exhibited immature/derailer Thinker traits.

_____

_____

_____

_____

Thinking back on this situation, what were the consequences of your immature actions? What happened?

_____

_____

_____

_____

When you acted immaturely, please describe in vivid detail the thoughts and feelings you experienced prior to taking the action you did.

_____

_____

_____

_____

Based on what you have read in this book and you reflecting on this situation, write a brief summary of how your thoughts, emotions, actions, and results were connected.

_____

_____

_____

_____

If this situation were to present itself again, what end result would you desire? Please provide vivid detail about the result, those who would most likely be impacted, and why they would be impacted. Please detail the who, what, when, where, why, and how associated with the end result you desire.

_____

_____

_____

_____

To achieve this new desired result, please indicate the actions and strategies you would take to ensure that the new desired end result would be achieved. Again, please detail the who, what, when, where, why, and how of your strategies. What stakeholders/mentors will you reach out to for their guidance, feedback, and support of your strategies?

_____

_____

_____

_____

To execute these actions and steps, what thoughts and emotions would need to be in place in order to support your positive actions?

_____

_____

_____

_____

After executing your new plan/strategy, what results were achieved and what did you learn?

_____

_____

_____

_____

CHAPTER

9

Understanding Your
Disciple Leadership Trait

Leaders who are predominant Disciples can sometimes appear incapable of action unless given permission from an authority figure, an institution, or a belief system. Thus, despite being in a leadership position, Disciples are often not the ones setting the tone, especially if they are derailing. Predominant Disciples can be the most puzzling because they can be highly reactive. They can fluctuate from one state to another at amazing speed and are notorious for reversing positions. They can be kind and understanding at one moment and vicious and unsympathetic the next moment. This instability is driven by the desire of Disciples not to be inferior. Because Disciples often need others to guide them, they constantly fear that they are inferior to their guiding force. After all, they reason to themselves, if one is fully capable, one would not need a guiding force. Over time, the guiding force of a Disciple may become a source of resentment for them because they are constantly being reminded of their inferiority. When this occurs, Disciples may behave both obediently and disobediently, simultaneously. Their desire to be told what to do compels them to be obedient, but their sense of inferiority compels them to be disobedient. Employees of derailing, predominant Disciples may never have a sense of what is expected of them. They may be told to do x when y occurs on one day, but to do z when y occurs on another day.

Mature, predominant Disciples, on the other hand, are able to form strong cohesive work groups. They tend to be down-to-earth and trustworthy, making it easy for others to open up to them. Mature, predominant Disciples have learned that loyalty shouldn't be directed only to the top. Consequently, mature, predominant Disciples are loyal to those they work with and form lasting bonds. This, in turn, inspires their own employees and team to be loyal and to work hard for them. As they derail, however, Disciples face increasing difficulty interacting with people. They become rigid and blindly follow rules. They spend more time enforcing rules and resenting those who break them than making rules and decisions. As explained, employees of derailing Disciples have difficulty knowing what to do and what is expected of them. They only know what not to do.

Like Thinkers, Disciples have problems dealing with their insecurities. Unfortunately, Disciples oscillate from feeling secure and confident to feeling insecure and unconfident. To minimize their feelings of insecurity, derailing Disciples offer their allegiance to an authority outside themselves. By having something bigger and more powerful to guide them, they feel protected. They no longer have to make decisions for themselves and can look to authorities to tell them what they can and cannot do. Despite any lingering reservations, Disciples remain silent and industrious. In essence, they do what they are told. Unfortunately, this does little to address the insecurities that haunt them or even the resentment they sometimes feel toward their authority figure.

Recognizing the Mature Disciple Trait in You
- Are disciplined, organized, responsible, and hardworking.
- Are down-to-earth and trustworthy.
- Identify strongly with others and form lasting bonds.
- Remain loyal to those you believe in.

- Work well in groups.
- Are capable of making effective decisions independently.

Recognizing the Middle-of-the-Road Mature Disciple in You
- Are afraid to make decisions and assume responsibility.
- Seek consultation when you are uncertain about what to do.
- Need reassurances when in difficult situations.
- Have low tolerance for ambiguity and need to know what is expected.
- Obey authority, even when the instructions are wrong.

Recognizing the Derailing Disciple in You
- Are stubborn and defensive.
- Are skeptical about people.
- Depend on authority and other people to make decisions for you.
- Resent those who break rules and get away with it.
- Fear being taken advantage of.
- Feel inferior.
- Complain about those who don't pull their weight.
- Procrastinate until pressure forces you to act.
- Can be volatile in high-pressure situations.

If you are a mature, predominant Disciple, in order to move toward increasing levels of leadership maturity, you need to follow the sequence presented on The Map as: 6 → 9 → 3. In other words, one of your objectives is to create a specific, compelling path that enables you to acquire and develop the mature traits of the Nine (Arbitrator). If this is you—the mature, predominant Disciple—you have learned to decrease your dependence on others. Additionally, you have learned to become more open, receptive, and sympathetic toward people. In essence, you are now able to support and reassure others, instead of seeking out reassurances and support for yourself. As you further cultivate the mature characteristics of predominant Arbitrators, your employees will see you as trustworthy and kindhearted. This, in turn, leads others to consider you for new opportunities, such as new challenges, projects, roles, and positions.

Derailing, predominant Disciples, on the other hand, when they are not spiraling toward greater maturity, run the risk of taking on even more immature characteristics, starting with the negative traits of the Three (Entertainer).

Your negative progression on The Map runs like this: 6 → 3 → 9. When derailing, predominant Disciples begin to acquire the derailing, predominant traits of the Entertainer, they stop turning their aggression inward and instead direct it outward toward others.

DISCIPLE LEADERSHIP STYLE

You tend not to seek out leadership positions. That said, when you are mature you can be very successful in a leadership role. In general, you tend to listen and ask questions rather than talk. When asked to take a stand, you can become tentative and indecisive. Others tend to view you—when derailing—as wishy-washy, tight-lipped, and unassertive. Additionally, others may see you as less confrontational, less demanding, and less competitive than other leadership types. Although many of these characteristics may suggest that you would not succeed in a leadership role, in fact, you possess the capability to be a highly effective leader when you focus on capitalizing and leveraging your strength and gifts. You are extraordinarily effective at providing structure to processes and systems. Your high need for security drives you to plan ahead and establish set patterns and procedures. This, in turn, gives your employees and teams a sense of security as well because they know that you are thinking ahead as evidenced through your clear expectations of them. You are also good at focusing other employees. You know how to complete tasks without being sidetracked and how to get others to do so as well. Despite being intensely task focused, you know how to have fun. When you are mature, you are easygoing, warm, accommodating, pleasant to work with, and driven to help people. You are also effective in identifying the unique needs of each of your employees and then tailoring a custom approach to help them satisfy their needs.

TIPS FOR STRENGTHENING THE DISCIPLE TRAIT IN YOU

- Look at things from a different angle. You often get into patterns where you believe that setbacks are permanent, pervasive, and personal. Reverse this pattern by affirming yourself and trying new approaches. After all, if you keep doing the same thing, you shouldn't expect different results.
- Become more trusting. You are good at getting people to like you, but your personal uncertainties prevent you from developing your

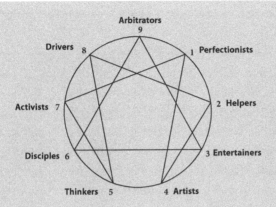

When *Disciple* leaders talk to themselves, here is what they say:

Basic Fear
I fear that I will be discarded if I don't follow along.

Basic Motivation
I want my position to be secure. I want others to like me so that my position will not be threatened.

My Greatest Irritation
I follow the rules and get irritated when others don't do the same. My irritation increases when those who don't follow the rules get away with it.

The Spark That Ignites My Defensiveness
I depend on others too much. I allow them to take responsibility for things I should be doing. I ask for permission for things I do not need permission for.

My Greatest Potential Weaknesses
I believe in the strength of others more than I believe in the strength of me.

My Greatest Strength
I am independent and confident. As I mature, I will trust myself and be confident in my ability to make decisions on my own. I will no longer need someone to watch over me or someone else to rely on.

relationships meaningfully. Letting people know how you feel about them allows you to build better relationships.

- Be more consistent in your interactions with people. What irritates others and undermines your relationships is that you often give mixed signals. Try being up-front and letting people know what is on your mind. This will stop the guesswork and clear up misunderstandings.
- Minimize your negative outbursts. You get edgy when you are upset and angry. When you are in a bad mood, resist the temptation to think negatively and whine. Even when you're having a bad day, don't try to make it a bad day for everyone else. Dragging everyone else down with you only builds resentment.
- Don't overreact under stress. You have a tendency to believe that the worst things will happen when you are stressed. When this occurs, think back to other times when you have been stressed. You'll probably find that your worst fears did not come true.
- Accept responsibility. People respect those who take responsibility for their actions, especially their mistakes. Blaming others for your failures will alienate you from others.
- Do not worship authority. Ingratiating yourself to someone in authority will get you nowhere in the long run. Those in power who want worshippers do not have your best interest at heart.

TIPS FOR WORKING WITH PREDOMINANT DISCIPLES

- Work with them one-on-one. When learning new things, Disciples favor one-on-one, hands-on instruction with real live human beings. You may need to take your time with Disciples because they want to observe each step until they are comfortable with doing it themselves. When learning, Disciples tend to observe others for longer than average amounts of time. Only when they feel confident that they will be able to perform a task successfully will they take the first step to begin.
- Be prepared to do more of the talking. Disciples are not comfortable in the spotlight and prefer to listen. When you first start to work with them, don't expect them to say much.
- Take your time. Disciples are risk averse, indecisive, and slow to make decisions. Consequently, you should not expect to make rapid

progress. Additionally, Disciples tend not to be forthcoming, so it may take some time to build trust and rapport with them. You may need to have questions ready in order to prompt them to talk. Remember that Disciples do not like sudden changes. It is better to introduce changes gradually rather than rapidly.

- Present clear instructions. When giving Disciples developmental exercises, giving easy-to-follow, specific, and clear instructions will produce better results. Disciples have trouble dealing with uncertainty. The more structure you can provide them, the less anxiety they will have with carrying out your instructions. Consequently, you should clearly lay out your expectations when you first meet with the Disciple.
- Praise specifics. When you provide feedback to Disciples, you should praise specific things they have done instead of abstract, personal attributes. Disciples tend to not be comfortable with overflowing praise.
- Focus on behaviors. Disciples are quick to become defensive and take things personally. By focusing on how you want to correct specific behaviors instead of on correcting them, you can help minimize their defensive reaction. If a behavior needs to be corrected, focus on offering suggestions for improvement instead of documenting everything they did wrong.

AWARENESS EXERCISE: BUILDING UP YOUR DISCIPLE TRAIT

In the spaces provided, please record your responses:

Provide a leadership example in which you exhibited immature/derailer Disciple traits.

_____

_____

_____

_____

Thinking back on this situation, what were the consequences of your immature actions? What happened?

_____

_____

_____

_____

When you acted immaturely, please describe in vivid detail the thoughts and feelings you experienced prior to taking the action you did.

_____

_____

_____

_____

Based on what you have read in this book and you reflecting on this situation, write a brief summary of how your thoughts, emotions, actions, and results were connected.

_____

_____

_____

_____

If this situation were to present itself again, what end result would you desire? Please provide vivid detail about the result, those who would most likely be impacted, and why they would be impacted. Please detail the who, what, when, where, why, and how associated with the end result you desire.

_____

_____

_____

_____

To achieve this new desired result, please indicate the actions and strategies you would take to ensure that the new desired end result would be achieved. Again, please detail the who, what, when, where, why, and how of your strategies. What stakeholders/mentors will you reach out to for their guidance, feedback, and support of your strategies?

_____

_____

_____

_____

To execute these actions and steps, what thoughts and emotions would need to be in place in order to support your positive actions?

_____

_____

_____

_____

After executing your new plan/strategy, what results were achieved and what did you learn?

_____

_____

_____

_____

CHAPTER

10

Understanding Your Activist Leadership Trait

Unlike the other predominant traits that comprise the Head triad—Thinkers who substitute thinking for doing and Disciples who have lost touch with their ability to act—the Activist overdoes everything. Activists are sensation seekers who are excited by their surroundings and who respond strongly to stimuli. The identity and self-esteem of Activists depend on obtaining a steady stream of sensations. Activists see themselves as happy and cheerful, but underneath their bright exterior can be a deep fear of pain. Derailing, predominant Activists are "afraid of the dark" and the painful side of reality, and they are well-known for changing the subject when serious issues arise. In short, they refuse to feel pain. To avoid pain, Activists seek to bury themselves in activities. At work, they can take on several projects and work long hours. Because they rarely slow down, fast-paced organizations are the ideal home for Activists.

Mature, predominant Activists are a great source of joy in the workplace and are good at doing many things at once. They are also extroverted, joyous, and positive; their mood becomes infectious, lifting the spirits of their employees and teams. In addition to being fun, mature predominant Activists are driven to produce something that can stimulate and provide joy to others. Because they possess and communicate a concrete vision of how they and their team can affect their environment, their employees can readily see how their actions align with this vision and contribute to a meaningful outcome. As they derail, however, Activists become obsessed with consuming more experiences. They don't care about producing something worthwhile. Instead, the organization and the people in the organization become a means of stimulation. The derailing, predominant Activist spends more time pursuing sensations that may or may not be productive. Derailing, predominant Activists demand instant gratification. If something occurs to them that they must do, they have to do it now! Employees, peers, and stakeholders find it difficult to work with derailing, predominant Activists because they always shift their priorities, and everything is an immediate priority. Long-term planning becomes impossible, and everyone is directed toward solving the crisis of the day. At their worst, derailing, predominant Activists can become manic; they start a million projects but complete none of them.

At their inner core, Activists have trouble dealing with their insecurities. Activists are not good at introspection and examining the causes of their anxiety. Derailing, predominant Activists respond to their insecurities by seeking out constant stimulation and activity to avoid dealing with the underlying causes of their fears. Unfortunately, the more activities they participate in to repress their fears, the less satisfying these experiences become. Eventually, they find little satisfaction in anything they do. When they realize they may never be satisfied, they can panic and become enraged at the world for failing to provide them the happiness they seek.

Recognizing the Mature Activist Trait in You

- Are spontaneous, enthusiastic, excitable, and exhilarated by activity.
- Are extroverted and highly responsive.
- Build relationships and seek out other people.

- Entertain others and can inspire with your storytelling.
- Appreciate the contributions of your employees and team.
- Focus on practical and productive solutions.
- Enjoy juggling many things at once.
- Can spot opportunities and are willing to take risks.
- See things to completion.

Recognizing the Middle-of-the-Road Mature Activist Trait in You

- Are materialistic, greedy, and superficial.
- Are loud, boisterous, and constantly talking.
- Constantly seek out new sensations and stimulation.
- Alienate people with your hyperactivity and flamboyance.
- Can juggle multiple things at once but have difficulty focusing on any one thing.
- Will start a million projects but seldom finish any.

Recognizing the Derailing Activist Trait in You

- Are impulsive and erratic and have little self-control.
- Become frustrated easily and quickly.
- Are prone to volatile mood swings and temper tantrums.
- Abuse others to get what you want.
- Strike out against those who get in your way.
- Disparage those who can't keep up with you.
- Constantly push the limits because you are never satisfied with what you have.

If you are a mature, predominant Activist, in order to move toward increasing levels of leadership maturity, you need to follow the sequence presented on The Map as: 7 → 5 → 8 → 2 → 4 → 1. In other words, your objective is to create a specific, compelling path that enables you to start to acquire and cultivate the mature attributes of the Five (Thinker). If this is you—a mature, predominant Activist—you have learned to dive beneath the surface and to know and truly understand more about the experiences that can bring joy to you. Instead of seeking out sensation, you now seek out real meaningful situations that bring you balance and joy. You now possess a richer, deeper understanding of the types of meaningful situations that can truly bring you balance and joy. This becomes the pathway to understanding what makes you happy and serves as a key step in your development. You have learned to stop looking outward for fulfillment; you now possess the ability of looking within as a source of building your balance and personal satisfaction. As a mature, predominant Activist, you now realize that your organization, as well as the people with whom you work and lead, are not there solely as a means to achieving greater personal fulfillment. Most importantly, you have learned to be introspective, analytical, and prudent before taking action.

Derailing, predominant Activists, on the other hand, when they are not spiraling toward greater maturity, run the risk of taking on even more immature characteristics, starting with the derailing traits of the One (Perfectionist). Your negative progression on The Map runs like this: $7 \rightarrow 1 \rightarrow 4 \rightarrow 2 \rightarrow 8 \rightarrow 5$. When derailing, predominant Activists are panic-stricken and out of control. By acquiring the derailing traits of the Perfectionist, they gain a false sense of control of their environment. Instead of diffusing their energy in a hundred different directions, they now focus their energy on one thing. They become fixated on perfecting this single thing and punish anyone who does not live up to their unobtainable standards. Although they now have a sense of direction, they are still no closer to feeling satisfied or fulfilled. As they become more unfulfilled, derailing, predominant Activists begin to resent others who are more fulfilled and endeavor to punish and bring them down.

ACTIVIST LEADERSHIP STYLE

When you are mature, you are good at lifting the spirits of your employees, teams, peers, and manager. You are both optimistic and confident. When things go wrong or people disappoint, you continue to remain optimistic. You handle criticism well and don't let the negative moods of others affect you. You view each new person and situation as interesting. This ability to make others feel unique and appreciated allows you to gain commitment from those you work with. You thrive when given multiple responsibilities and seek out a variety of activities and projects. You may falter in situations with little variety and routine activities. You tend to seek out opportunities that provide you freedom, power, and materialistic rewards. When derailing, anything that is confining and restrictive can make you feel uncomfortable; you tend to have bitter feelings toward anyone whom you perceive has held you back. As a leader, you give considerable freedom to your employees and team as you prefer a hands-off

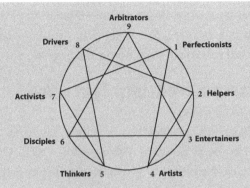

When *Activist* leaders talk to themselves, here's what they say:

Basic Fear
I fear being deprived of what I deserve.

Basic Motivation
I want to be fulfilled and satisfied. I want to have fun with what I am doing.

My Greatest Irritation
I get upset when someone or something prevents me from getting what I want.

The Spark That Ignites My Defensiveness
I believe that I will be happier if I have more of everything and accomplish as much as possible. Unfortunately, as I attempt to get more, I only increase the size of my appetite without really satisfying it.

My Greatest Potential Weakness
I want too many experiences as opposed to fewer but more satisfying experiences.

My Greatest Potential Strength
I am appreciative of what I have. As I grow and mature, I will value the experiences that I have instead of constantly searching for new ones.

approach. You also tend to be direct and open when working with your employees, team, and stakeholders. You prefer to be on a first-name basis, and you desire close, personal relationships at home and at work.

TIPS FOR STRENGTHENING THE ACTIVIST TRAIT IN YOU

- Try not to be so impulsive.
- Learn to say no. You don't have to do everything. Good opportunities will come back again if you perform well. If you don't say no and take on hundreds of projects, your performance on all of your projects will suffer. By picking and choosing where you apply your energy, you will perform better.
- Select quality over quantity. Doing a few things well is better than doing many things poorly.
- Think about the future. Before deciding on what you want now, think about what you want in the future. Does your decision at this moment put you on the path you want to be on down the line?
- Learn to listen to other people. You don't have to be the life of every party. People are interesting, and you can learn a lot if you give them a chance to talk. Remember that people don't like those who never shut up.
- Think about the details. As a big-picture thinker, you tend to gloss over details. However, for plans to be effective, details are necessary. Take time to be more objective in your analysis and learn to attend to facts.

TIPS FOR WORKING WITH PREDOMINANT ACTIVISTS

- Be entertaining and fast-moving. Activists are sensation seekers, and the best way to reach them is by working with them at a quick pace.
- Be bold. Activists like people who are direct and express themselves. You should bring up topics openly.
- Frame things as an opportunity or challenge. As optimists, Activists do not want to deal with problems. By framing problems as opportunities, you can get Activists to approach the issue. Framing a problem as a problem only repels Activists.
- Use stories and testimonials. Activists tend not to be influenced by statistics and facts. Using stories and illustrations that relate to them and their goals is a better way of influencing them.

- Give them the big picture. Activists tend to be big-picture thinkers. After seeing the broad overview, Activists have little interest in getting tied down to specifics. Just remember that Activists want adventure, not analysis. Provide them with broad overviews of options and alternatives. You should paint a picture of the future state of affairs with each alternative. Provide testimonials after they decided on an alternative. If you give testimonials too soon, Activists will interpret it as a sign that you are trying to restrict their freedom and they will fight you.
- Read their expressions. Activists tend to regulate their outward expression less than other personality types; they are open books. To see where you stand, just look at their faces.
- Allow Activists time to vent. With all that is going on in their life, Activists sometimes need time to vent their feelings. When this occurs, listen for facts and feelings and probe with direct questions.
- Be clear and specific about what you expect. Activists tend not to think about things too deeply. If you have an objective for them to meet, you need to tell them directly instead of hoping for them to figure it out on their own. Activists are too busy to ponder what your hidden motives are. Involving them with agreeing on expectations and strategies will result in greater buy-in. You will need to establish checkpoints to prevent Activists from going off on tangents.
- Write things down and prioritize. Activists tend to have so many things going on that they forget to finish tasks on time or procrastinate until the last minute, putting out the latest fire. By having a record of what they need to do and for whom, you can help Activists better prioritize their time. You should summarize what has been agreed to in writing. Otherwise, the Activist may forget and focus on handling the latest crisis.
- Don't frame schedules as a loss of freedom. With so many commitments, Activists benefit from having a schedule. However, many Activists view a schedule as a loss of freedom. You should discuss how a schedule is not a loss of freedom if the Activist creates the schedule him- or herself.

AWARENESS EXERCISE: BUILDING UP YOUR ACTIVIST TRAIT

In the spaces provided, please record your responses:

Provide a leadership example in which you exhibited immature/derailer Activist traits.

_____

_____

_____

_____

Thinking back on this situation, what were the consequences of your immature actions? What happened?

_____

_____

_____

_____

When you acted immaturely, please describe in vivid detail the thoughts and feelings you experienced prior to taking the action you did.

_____

_____

_____

_____

Based on what you have read in this book and you reflecting on this situation, write a brief summary of how your thoughts, emotions, actions, and results were connected.

_____

_____

_____

_____

If this situation were to present itself again, what end result would you desire? Please provide vivid detail about the result, those who would most likely be impacted, and why they would be impacted. Please detail the who, what, when, where, why, and how associated with the end result you desire.

_____

_____

_____

_____

To achieve this new desired result, please indicate the actions and strategies you would take to ensure that the new desired end result would be achieved. Again, please detail the who, what, when, where, why, and how of your strategies. What stakeholders/mentors will you reach out to for their guidance, feedback, and support of your strategies?

_____

_____

_____

_____

To execute these actions and steps, what thoughts and emotions would need to be in place in order to support your positive actions?

_____

_____

_____

_____

After executing your new plan/strategy, what results were achieved and what did you learn?

_____

_____

_____

_____

CHAPTER
11

Understanding Your
Driver Leadership Trait

Leaders who are predominant Drivers are perhaps the most openly aggressive leaders of all. Drivers are take-charge people who enjoy imposing their will on the environment, which includes other people. Drivers gravitate toward leadership positions as a way to control their environments. They can be difficult to deal with because getting what they want is so critical to them. Drivers tend to be larger than life and make their presence felt. You can't help but pay attention to them. When they rumble into a room, you know they've arrived. Drivers notice when other people notice them. They like the attention. In fact, much of their seemingly endless supply of energy comes from the reactions they generate from others.

When they are mature, Drivers use their immense self-confidence and will to make things better. Mature Drivers believe in causes other than themselves and can inspire others to adopt their causes. Drivers have an indomitable will and persist until they have achieved their goals. As long as their egos are kept in check, their behaviors benefit others. Derailing Drivers have no cause other than themselves. They seek to acquire power and to prevail over others simply for the sake of overcoming them and asserting their will. Derailing Drivers can be especially dangerous because they don't realize how insensitive they are; they gain a great deal of satisfaction by constantly trying to dominate others.

The central problem facing Drivers is their overdeveloped relatedness to their environment. Drivers are constantly comparing themselves to other people. Drivers believe they are better than everyone else. This is why Drivers are so driven to dominate their environments. They believe that because they are the best, they should naturally make the decisions. Unfortunately, when this does not occur, Drivers often become frustrated over their lack of standing in the world. This disconnect between their inflated sense of self and their actual standing in the world becomes too much to bear. Derailing Drivers become hostile and ruthless. Anyone else who is doing better than them or who has higher social standing is viewed as a threat and becomes a source of resentment. As leaders, derailing Drivers tend to be little more than egomaniacs. They pit themselves and others loyal to them against rivals in struggles for power and dominance. Derailing Drivers spend so much time and energy fighting for the right to lead that they don't actually lead people in fruitful directions. Derailing Drivers are especially dangerous in positions of power because they direct so many resources toward internal squabbles that they fail to notice threats external to the organization. In essence, Drivers may end up spending so much time fighting to lead that they destroy the organization they are trying to lead.

Recognizing the Mature Driver Trait in You

- Are assertive, self-confident, and decisive.
- Are a resourceful self-starter with contagious energy and enthusiasm.
- Win the respect and admiration of others.
- Provide, sponsor, and promote worthwhile causes.
- Inspire others to act.
- Align your interests with others.
- Tend to be viewed as heroic by others.

Recognizing the Middle-of-the-Road Mature Driver Trait in You
- Are forceful, aggressive, confrontational, and belligerent.
- Are adventurous and willing to take risks in order to dominate your environment.
- Care only about your own interests and use your power to promote your own self-interest.
- Seek to dominate your environment regardless of the cost to others.
- Enjoy keeping others off balance and insecure.
- Often use threats and fear to gain compliance from others.
- Can be egomaniacal.

Recognizing the Derailing Driver Trait in You
- Are ruthless and dictatorial.
- Are immoral and without guilt.
- Believe in survival of the fittest.
- Feel invincible and do not fear others.
- Will behave recklessly to get what you want.
- Can be hostile and violent.

If you are a mature, predominant Driver, in order to move toward increasing levels of leadership maturity, you need to follow the sequence presented on The Map as: 8 → 2 → 4 → 1 → 7 → 5. In other words, one of your objectives is to create a specific, compelling path that enables you to start to acquire and cultivate the mature attributes of the Two (Helper). If this is you—a mature, predominant Driver—you have learned to use your power and influence for others rather than against them. You have learned to be caring, generous, and personally concerned. By identifying with others, you have learned a key developmental lesson: *All people are worthy of the same rights and privileges that you seek for yourself.*

Derailing, predominant Drivers, on the other hand, when they are not spiraling toward greater maturity, run the risk of acquiring even more immature characteristics, starting with the derailing traits of the Five (Thinker). Your negative progression on The Map runs like this: 8 → 5 → 7 → 1 → 4 → 2. Instead of acting belligerently, the derailing, predominant Driver now becomes more tactical but in a negative way. Although they actually may become less reckless, unfortunately, they also become more secretive, and they will strike without warning. By becoming more withdrawn, they are able to hide from their enemies and create detailed plans designed to attack and weaken them. Their motto? "I don't get mad. I get even!"

DRIVER LEADERSHIP STYLE

As a leader, you are intensely task focused. It isn't that you aren't warm, friendly, or personable. Your priority is to get things done—well. You are good at both starting and finishing projects. You are also capable of juggling multiple responsibilities simultaneously. In turn, you expect the same level of drive and ability from your employees and teams. When you perceive that the output from others is less than exemplary, your reaction is swift and direct: "Do something!" When derailing, you can be so strong-willed and goal oriented that you will almost sacrifice everything to achieve your objectives. In addition, when derailing, you are willing to put in long hours, and sometimes your personal and social lives fall apart from neglect in your quest to accumulate work-related achievements. This intense commitment can become a source of conflict between you and your employees if they are unwilling to dedicate as much to work. If you are derailing, you may have difficulty delegating tasks and difficulty admitting that you are unable to do everything all of the time.

TIPS FOR STRENGTHENING THE DRIVER TRAIT IN YOU

- Remember that you are not the only person in the world. Others have the same needs and rights as you. Ignoring or violating their rights will lead them to fear you, hate you, and turn against you.
- Act with more self-restraint. When you are successful, don't go out of your way to crush people. Showing mercy and restraint wins more respect and loyalty than demonstrating your raw power.
- Learn to let others win. When little is at stake, you can afford to let others have their way. By creating opportunities for others, they will create opportunities for you down the line.
- Involve others in goal setting and problem solving. You don't know everything, and by including others, you can develop more realistic goals and better solutions.
- Realize that no one is self-sufficient. Although you want to be self-reliant and independent, you must recognize that cooperation with others is necessary to achieve your goals.

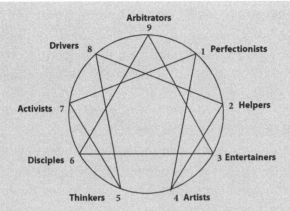

When *Driver* leaders talk to themselves, here's what they say:

Basic Fear
I fear submitting to others.

Basic Motivation
I want control over my environment and the respect of others. I want people to listen to me. I want to be self-reliant.

My Greatest Irritation
I know others out there would take advantage of me if I let them.

The Spark That Ignites My Defensiveness
I believe that I'm entirely self-sufficient.

My Greatest Potential Weakness
I lust for power and the ability to control others.

My Greatest Potential Strength
I am a generous person. When I mature, I will take the needs of others into equal consideration and make sure they win as well.

- Find a higher purpose. Many Drivers place too much value on money and other material signs of achievement. Having a nonmaterial goal allows you to feel more fulfilled. Additionally, other people tend to be more inspired by nonmaterial goals. By having a calling, you can gain greater influence.

TIPS FOR WORKING WITH PREDOMINANT DRIVERS

- Indicate how you can help Drivers achieve their objectives. If Drivers perceive you as useless to achieving their goals, they will eliminate you. You need to indicate all you can do and would like to do to achieve Drivers' objectives.
- Keep things businesslike. Drivers are focused on achieving tangible goals. They are not there to make friends. If you spend time trying to build a personal relationship, the Driver will interpret this as a waste of time. Only try to build a personal relationship if the Driver indicates that this is the objective.
- Avoid personality conflicts. If you have a disagreement with the Driver, focus on the facts, not on the person. Because Drivers believe they are better than everyone else, criticizing their personal characteristics will set them off and make them defensive.
- Ask specific questions. Drivers want to get things done. Focusing on concrete actions and results that must take place for Drivers to achieve their goals is the best way to influence them.
- If you can't agree with the conclusions of a Driver, explain directly why you can't agree and indicate what actions you see as realistic alternatives.

AWARENESS EXERCISE: BUILDING UP YOUR DRIVER TRAIT

In the spaces provided, please record your responses:

Provide a leadership example in which you exhibited immature/derailer Driver traits.

_____

_____

_____

_____

Thinking back on this situation, what were the consequences of your immature actions? What happened?

_____

_____

_____

_____

When you acted immaturely, please describe in vivid detail the thoughts and feelings you experienced prior to taking the action you did.

_____

_____

_____

_____

Based on what you have read in this book and you reflecting on this situation, write a brief summary of how your thoughts, emotions, actions, and results were connected.

_____

_____

_____

_____

If this situation were to present itself again, what end result would you desire? Please provide vivid detail about the result, those who would most likely be impacted, and why they would be impacted. Please detail the who, what, when, where, why, and how associated with the end result you desire.

_____

_____

_____

_____

To achieve this new desired result, please indicate the actions and strategies you would take to ensure the new desired end result would be achieved. Again, please detail the who, what, when, where, why, and how of your strategies. What stakeholders/mentors will you reach out to for their guidance, feedback, and support of your strategies?

_____

_____

_____

_____

To execute these actions and steps, what thoughts and emotions would need to be in place in order to support your positive actions?

_____

_____

_____

_____

After executing your new plan/strategy, what results were achieved and what did you learn?

_____

_____

_____

_____

CHAPTER
12

Understanding Your
Arbitrator Leadership Trait

Leaders who are predominant Arbitrators tend to be the most open of all types. What you see with the Arbitrator is what you get. Arbitrators are likable because they get along with mostly anyone. Unlike Drivers, who seek to dominate their environment, Arbitrators seek to coexist with it. They are adaptable to almost any environment and situation. Rather than creating conflict, Arbitrators identify common ground and find ways to bring people together. When mature, Arbitrators excel at finding common ground; when derailing, however, they are not particularly good at determining what they want or in directing other people. Employees and teams often become frustrated at the inability of derailing, predominant Arbitrator leaders to establish a clear path or vision.

Mature, predominant Arbitrators excel in involving everyone. Their easygoing yet emphatic demeanor makes it easy for people to open up to them. The highly developed listening skills of Arbitrators also make them easy people to disclose information to. Because people trust them, Arbitrators tend to end up as a central component in social networks. In essence, people feel comfortable with Arbitrators and go to them for a sympathetic ear. These skills make mature, predominant Arbitrators particularly effective mediators. If there is conflict, Arbitrators can resolve it and bring warring parties together. As they derail, however, Arbitrators may abdicate, even neglect their responsibilities. Instead of dealing with problems, they walk away from them. Derailing, predominant Arbitrators often have trouble focusing and believe that little they do truly matters. People stop going to a derailing, predominant Arbitrator because they realize that the Arbitrator can be paralyzed by inaction.

The central problem facing Arbitrators is that they are out of touch with their relatedness to their environment. Although Arbitrators can adapt and fit into any environment, when derailing, they don't really feel as though they belong. In essence, Arbitrators can have a hard time finding a purpose and mission in life. Sometimes they fail to see anything as important. This leads Arbitrators to undertake many projects but invest little energy in any of them. For this reason, many people see derailing, predominant Arbitrators as lazy or uncommitted. Their inability to devote energy to specific projects or goals often sends a destructive signal to others. Employees correctly interpret the lack of clear direction they are receiving as a lack of motivation on their leader's part. This, in turn, undermines the Arbitrator's ability to create passion and drive in their people.

Recognizing the Mature Arbitrator Trait in You

- Are easygoing, empathetic, and supportive.
- Are a good listener and mediator.
- Excellent facilitator, capable of uniting diverse groups together.
- Accept yourself and others.
- Know what you want and value.

Recognizing the Middle-of-the-Road Mature Arbitrator in You

- Are submissive and passive.
- Are inattentive, unreflective, and stoic.

- Fear change.
- Have difficulty focusing, with a tendency to procrastinate.
- Walk away from problems.
- Look for magical solutions rather than depend on ordinary judgment.

Recognizing the Derailing Arbitrator Trait in You
- Are repressed to the point of helplessness.
- Are obstinate to the point of denial.
- Are neglectful to the point of irresponsibility.
- Avoid problems and conflicts.
- Do not want to do anything.

If you are a mature, predominant Arbitrator, in order to move toward increasing levels of leadership maturity, you need to follow the sequence presented on The Map as: 9 → 3 → 6. In other words, one of your objectives is to create a specific, compelling development path that enables you to acquire and develop the mature attributes of the Three (Entertainer). If this is you—a mature, predominant Arbitrator—you have become more self-assured and interested in developing yourself to your fullest potential. Mature, predominant Arbitrators, who acquire the mature traits of the Entertainer, devote energy to discovering who they are and finding where they fit in the world. Instead of trying to live up to the expectations of others, they finally live up to their own expectations. They know what they want and become more assertive in their relationships with other people.

Derailing, predominant Arbitrators, on the other hand, when they are not spiraling toward greater maturity, run the risk of acquiring even more immature characteristics starting with the derailing traits of the Six (Disciple). Your negative progression on The Map runs like this: 9 → 6 → 3. The repressed anxiety Arbitrators feel regarding their inability to find a purpose in life comes crashing through. Arbitrators cease being easygoing and can become hysterical, anxiety ridden, fearful, agitated, and apprehensive. In this state, derailing, predominant Arbitrators have difficulty in managing themselves, let alone in managing others.

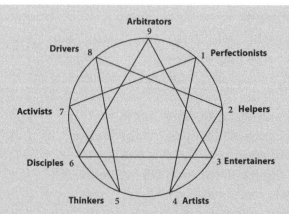

When *Arbitrator* leaders talk to themselves, here's what they say:

Basic Fear
I fear being disconnected from others.

Basic Motivation
I want peace and harmony. I want to bring people together and end conflict.

My Greatest Irritation
I don't like it when people try to force me to change.

The Spark That Ignites My Defensiveness
I think I am nice to others and maintain relationships, but others see me as passive and neglectful of important problems.

My Greatest Potential Weakness
I can be slow, lazy, and indifferent to problems.

My Greatest Potential Strength
I am patient. I believe that by leaving things alone, they will run their course without needing any interference from me.

ARBITRATOR LEADERSHIP STYLE

When you are mature, you are well suited for leadership positions because of your highly developed planning skills and ability to get along with people. As a leader, you seek to create stability. You want to have conflict-free relationships with others. The desire for stability leads you to have a high regard for tradition and routine. As a leader, you clearly define the roles and responsibilities of each employee. You seek to create a harmonious and finely tuned orchestra, with each employee playing a key role. You face difficulty when tried-and-true methods no longer work. In short, situations that require innovative and revolutionary changes can discomfort you. When mature, you tend to be well liked by your employees because of your immodesty and accommodating style. You are not as in-your-face as other leadership types. You would rather not make waves, and you think that your actions should speak for themselves. Despite these positive characteristics, derailing, predominant Arbitrators do face challenges as leaders. If this is you, your desire to maintain a conflict-free workplace makes it difficult to criticize or discipline your employees and team. You may avoid disciplining your employees to the point that you lose credibility. Additionally, your modest nature makes it difficult for people to identify with you or view you as heroic figures.

TIPS FOR STRENGTHENING THE ARBITRATOR TRAIT IN YOU

- Know your limits, and don't go beyond them. Your desire to keep peace makes you vulnerable to bending over backward for others. Identify the things you are unwilling to compromise on, and don't compromise on those things. By knowing where you draw the line, you will be less vulnerable to being taken advantage of.
- Be more assertive. You should continue to pay attention to the needs of others, but you need to pay more attention to your needs.
- Be more open. Try to break from your routine from time to time. You may discover better ways of doing things, and greater variety will increase your satisfaction.
- Share your feelings with trusted friends. By discussing your feelings, you will be less influenced by them. You need to have confidence that you will not damage your relationships with others by being human.
- Share something about yourself. People naturally feel safe and comfortable around you. This leads others to disclose a lot to you.

Remember to share a little about yourself as well. By doing this, you build even more trust because people will no longer think you are holding back.

Tips for Working with Predominant Arbitrators

- Encourage Arbitrators to be more straightforward. Arbitrators prefer to use indirect and subtle approaches when sharing their expectations, ideas, or reactions. This often leads them to be ignored or misinterpreted. Tell Arbitrators that they have valuable ideas and that they should be expressed. You can also encourage Arbitrators to open up by asking them open-ended questions that can't be answered with a single word or gesture.
- Help Arbitrators monitor their tendency to tolerate others to the point of becoming their victims. You must remind Arbitrators that they have personal lines that shouldn't be crossed and that there are limits to how much they should accommodate people.
- Set time limits. Because Arbitrators tend to be indirect, they tend to take longer to get to the point. By having a time limit, it forces the Arbitrator to get to the main point.
- Create a schedule and get them to accept it. The natural optimism of Arbitrators may delude them into underestimating the time it takes to complete a project. Work with Arbitrators, and get them to commit to specific deadlines, objectives, and constraints.

AWARENESS EXERCISE: BUILDING UP YOUR ARBITRATOR TRAIT

In the spaces provided, please record your responses:

Provide a leadership example in which you exhibited immature/derailer Arbitrator traits.

_____

_____

_____

_____

Thinking back on this situation, what were the consequences of your immature actions? What happened?

_____

_____

_____

_____

When you acted immaturely, please describe in vivid detail the thoughts and feelings you experienced prior to taking the action you did.

_____

_____

_____

_____

Based on what you have read in this book and you reflecting on this situation, write a brief summary of how your thoughts, emotions, actions, and results were connected.

_____

_____

_____

_____

If this situation were to present itself again, what end result would you desire? Please provide vivid detail about the result, those who would most likely be impacted, and why they would be impacted. Please detail the who, what, when, where, why, and how associated with the end result you desire.

_____

_____

_____

_____

To achieve this new desired result, please indicate the actions and strategies you would take to ensure the new desired end result would be achieved. Again, please detail the who, what, when, where, why, and how of your strategies. What stakeholders/mentors will you reach out to for their guidance, feedback, and support of your strategies?

_____

_____

_____

_____

To execute these actions and steps, what thoughts and emotions would need to be in place in order to support your positive actions?

_____

_____

_____

_____

After executing your new plan/strategy, what results were achieved and what did you learn?

_____

_____

_____

_____

CHAPTER

13

Understanding Your
Perfectionist Leadership Trait

Leaders who are predominant Perfectionists endeavor to perfect everything in their environment. This desire for perfection extends to themselves and other people. Perfectionists are highly critical of themselves and others. Their favorite words are *should* and *must*. Because nothing is perfect, Perfectionists become disappointed by reality. As their disappointments inevitably pile up, their frustrations mutate into a universal rage at the imperfect state of the world. This anger supplies Perfectionists with boundless energy to improve the world as they see it. Unfortunately, an aggressive, negative energy threatens to consume the Perfectionist. As powerful as their rage is, it doesn't look like rage. At first glance, it is easy to mistake it for zeal or idealism. Perfectionists themselves may not know they are angry at the world because their anger is masked behind high ideals and noble goals. It is easy for Perfectionists to win people over initially to their cause. Other people become enticed by their character and conviction. Over time, the same people who flocked to the Perfectionist's cause often flee it. Others begin to realize that the dreams of Perfectionists are impossible to achieve and that there is no pleasing them. Although there may be a revolving door of converts, Perfectionists often pay no attention to those who flee. In their minds, the deserters were never worthy in the first place. However, truly derailed Perfectionists may go out of their way to punish those who abandon their cause. Their sense of perfection cannot tolerate the idea that they may be wrong.

Mature, predominant Perfectionists are capable of being highly noble leaders. With their deep sense of right and wrong and ethical principles, other employees know that Perfectionists can be relied upon. Mature, predominant Perfectionists earn the trust of both employees and customers because of their unwillingness to cut corners. Mature, predominant Perfectionists are also good decision makers. They are impartial, fair, and objective in their dealings with people. They don't play favorites and side with those who have the best plan. Mature, predominant Perfectionists are also in touch with their humanity. They tolerate their own and other people's shortcomings. Although mature, predominant Perfectionists desire perfection, they acknowledge that it is impossible and are satisfied with achieving high-quality standards. For instance, they realize that it is better to deliver a product with a quality rating between 90 and 95 percent, on time, than it is to deliver a product with a quality rating of 100 percent that is six months to a year late.

As they derail, Perfectionists become completely consumed by their desire to achieve perfection. Their objectives become their singular focus. Derailing, predominant Perfectionists become increasingly inflexible and dogmatic. They believe that their way is the only right way and refuse to listen to anyone else. They belittle and attack anyone and everyone who thinks differently. At the end, their projects tend to be overbudget, late, and of lower quality. Instead of achieving perfection, derailing, predominant Perfectionists have made things worse and driven people away.

The central problem facing Perfectionists is their underdeveloped relatedness with others and their environment. Perfectionists often fail to see human beings as human beings. In essence, people are just pieces of the environmental puzzle waiting to be perfected. This dehumanization of people also extends to themselves. Perfectionists spend so much time trying to perfect themselves and others that they fail to take into account their own or other people's needs. They spend so much time seeing people's faults that they fail to notice their strengths. In their quest to make people better, Perfectionists can be brutal and sadistic in their treatment of other people. They either fail to notice the suffering of others or justify their suffering as necessary to achieving perfection.

Recognizing the Mature Perfectionist Trait in You
- Are satisfied with achieving 80–95 percent of your original goals.
- Are good at evaluating problems and determining priorities.
- Are conscientious and self-disciplined.
- Are highly principled and ethical.
- Have a deep sense of right and wrong, placing high value on truth and justice.
- Have realistic goals instead of unattainable goals.
- Can be relied upon to be impartial, fair, and objective.
- Tolerate your own and others' shortcomings.
- Feel good about yourself if you put forth a good effort, even if the outcome isn't perfect.

Recognizing the Middle-of-the-Road Mature Perfectionist in You
- Are logical, orderly, and idealistic.
- Can be rigid, impersonal, and emotionally constricted.
- Fear making mistakes.
- Frequently experience guilt and anxiety for failing to achieve perfection.
- Badger others to improve their imperfect states.
- Try to be excellent at everything.
- Are driven by the words *should* and *must*.

Recognizing the Derailing Perfectionist in You
- Are dogmatic and inflexible.
- Believe you are never wrong and always have to be right.
- Believe you are perfect.
- Have unattainable ideals and are impossible to please or satisfy.
- Rationalize your actions to maintain your "logical" position.
- Can be cruel and sadistic.
- Enjoy proving others wrong.

If you are a mature, predominant Perfectionist, in order to move toward increasing levels of leadership maturity, you need to follow the sequence presented on The Map as: 1 → 7 → 5 → 8 → 2 → 4. In other words, one of your objectives is to create a specific, compelling development path that enables you to acquire and develop the mature attributes of the Seven (Activist). If this is you—a mature, predominant Perfectionist—you have learned to relax and enjoy life. Although acknowledging that you are not perfect, you are comforted knowing and accepting that you are as capable, if not more capable, than other people. Freed of the straightjacket of the never-ending pursuit of perfection, you have learned to become comfortable in your own skin. With increasing maturity, you become less serious and learn to joke around. Instead of seeing people as objects to be perfected, you begin to see people as unique individuals, each with something to offer. This new focus on building relationships enables you not only to be more fulfilled, but to achieve greater success through working with others. You have learned to stop focusing on the "best" solution and instead focus on practical solutions. You become more flexible and use different approaches to solve problems.

Derailing, predominant Perfectionists, on the other hand, when not spiraling toward greater maturity, run the risk of acquiring even more immature characteristics, starting with the derailing traits of the Four (Artist). Your negative progression on The Map runs like this: 1 → 4 → 2 → 8 → 5 → 7. Derailing, predominant Perfectionists begin to realize that their never-ending pursuit of unobtainable ideals is futile. By ruthlessly pursuing their ideals, they have alienated themselves from others. Without any meaningful connections and with letdowns mounting, derailing, predominant Perfectionists realize they have failed. Instead of setting more realistic goals and being nicer to people, they give up. They become depressed, overly negative, and angry at themselves. Because they can't achieve perfection, they don't see the point of anything. Whereas they once sought power to change the world into their idealized image, derailing, predominant Perfectionists seek to avoid any form of responsibility. They further remove themselves from people and wallow in their self-pity.

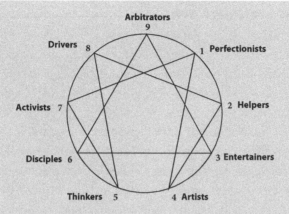

When *Perfectionist* leaders talk to themselves, here's what they say:

Basic Fear
I fear being proved wrong.

Basic Motivation
I want to improve the world. By controlling everything, I can ensure that no mistakes are made.

My Greatest Irritation
I am right most of the time. It really upsets me when people don't listen to me. If they listened to me, things would have worked out better.

The Spark That Ignites My Defensiveness
I believe that I am the only one capable of improving the world. If I don't do it, no one else will.

My Greatest Potential Weakness
I have a lot of self-righteous anger. I become frustrated with all the flaws around me. This anger sometimes builds until I reach a boiling point and lash out at people.

My Greatest Potential Strength
I become wiser as I mature. I will then be able to know when something is good enough and will stop working on it before diminishing returns kick in and additional effort contributes little improvement.

PERFECTIONIST LEADERSHIP STYLE

When you are mature, you are an excellent planner and good at fostering quality-oriented cultures. You see yourself, as others do, as a problem solver. You are good at identifying key issues, seeing critical details, and asking specific questions. Because you see yourself as having the best ideas, you seek out positions of influence. You have an innate desire to know how things work. You are immensely process oriented and care as much about how goals are accomplished as you do about whether goals are accomplished. Your process orientation allows you to identify areas of improvement. As a leader, you focus on continuous improvement. Every step, every procedure can and must be improved. Your desire to achieve perfection leads you to sometimes overplan. You enjoy planning for every contingency and often have a plan B, plan C, and so on. You even incorporate extra time in your schedule to accommodate for expected last-minute glitches. Your risk-averse nature leads you to check, double-check, and triple-check things. If derailing, you sometimes lose focus on what is critical. You can focus so much on details that you lose sight of the big picture. Because of this tendency, you may also hold up projects to make subtle tweaks in your attempt to inch projects toward perfection. Another challenge that you face is your inclination for objects rather than people. Because people are unpredictable, complicated, and difficult to understand, when derailing, you may seek to avoid them. Perhaps the most important key to success for you and your leadership style is to learn to abandon your quest for perfection and settle for mere excellence.

TIPS FOR STRENGTHENING THE PERFECTIONIST TRAIT IN YOU

- Learn to relax. Your desire for continuous improvement makes you very intense, which can scare off a lot of people. Recognize that the world around you will not crumble if you don't fix it right this moment. Try to be content with being merely excellent. Slowing down will allow you to appreciate your accomplishments.
- Learn to listen to others. You don't know everything, and your coworkers may have valuable insights. By listening to others, you can achieve greater success and move closer to your goals of perfection.
- Take time with people. What is obvious to you may not be obvious to others. By being patient with people, you earn their respect. Lashing out at them for not getting something earns only their resentment and contempt.

- Recognize that there is more than one "right" way. You often get angry when others don't behave as you expect them to. You need to recognize that your definition of the right way may be different from someone else's. You both may be right, and there may be multiple ways to do something correctly.
- Remember that you are not perfect. Try not to criticize others as much, and remember that you have faults and shortcomings as well.
- Stop trying to be perfect. Your impossibly high standards drive people crazy and hinder your ability to meet deadlines. Learn to accept less. You do not have to be perfect to be good

TIPS FOR WORKING WITH PREDOMINANT PERFECTIONISTS

- Get Perfectionists to interact with other personality types. More so than other personality types, Perfectionists need to be encouraged to branch out and interact with others. Perfectionists tend to be introverted and prefer to work with other Perfectionists. To develop them further, you need to get them to interact with other personality types. Tell them that, through interacting with other personality types, they will be better able to understand and influence them. By framing these interactions as developmental exercises that will bring them closer to being the perfect leader, you will motivate Perfectionists to try. Through interacting with other personality types, you will be able to round off some of the rough edges of the Perfectionist. For example, Drivers can help Perfectionists maintain deadlines, and Entertainers can help Perfectionists lighten up.
- Teach Perfectionists the importance of acting at 90 percent. Perfectionists don't like to make decisions until they have 100 percent of the information and are certain they are correct. Unfortunately, it is seldom the case that anyone has all the information. By waiting until they are absolutely certain, Perfectionists may miss out on time-limited opportunities. It is critical that you teach Perfectionists the importance of acting on good information, instead of waiting on complete information. By delaying action, Perfectionists may miss out on opportunities with narrow windows.
- Persuade Perfectionists to limit the number of alternatives they consider. Perfections are notorious for paralyzing themselves through

the generation of too many alternatives. It is difficult to determine the best course of action when there are 10 to 20 possibilities. Force Perfectionists to limit their choices to two alternatives. Having more than two choices may immobilize them.

- Focus on quality over quantity. The best way to influence Perfectionists is to focus on quality. Perfectionists are not impressed by a high number of mediocre products or services.
- Support your statements and proposals. Perfectionists are detail oriented and will rip apart your coaching plans if there is insufficient supporting evidence to back up your claims. They don't accept things on faith alone.
- Control the time frame. Perfectionists will delay everything to perfect things further. By having hard deadlines that don't budge, you can help convince Perfectionists of the importance of producing good enough products within a deadline versus perfect products that are late. The products that Perfectionists deliver at the deadline will likely be high quality, even if they can't see that. Perfectionists must learn that if they constantly delay things to perfect them, they will never achieve anything.

AWARENESS EXERCISE: BUILDING UP YOUR PERFECTIONIST TRAIT

In the spaces provided, please record your responses:

Provide a leadership example in which you exhibited immature/derailer Perfectionist traits.

_____

_____

_____

_____

Thinking back on this situation, what were the consequences of your immature actions? What happened?

_____

_____

_____

_____

When you acted immaturely, please describe in vivid detail the thoughts and feelings you experienced prior to taking the action you did.

_____

_____

_____

_____

Based on what you have read in this book and you reflecting on this situation, write a brief summary of how your thoughts, emotions, actions, and results were connected.

_____

_____

_____

_____

If this situation were to present itself again, what end result would you desire? Please provide vivid detail about the result, those who would most likely be impacted, and why they would be impacted. Please detail the who, what, when, where, why, and how associated with the end result you desire.

_____

_____

_____

_____

To achieve this new desired result, please indicate the actions and strategies you would take to ensure that the new desired end result would be achieved. Again, please detail the who, what, when, where, why, and how of your strategies. What stakeholders/mentors will you reach out to for their guidance, feedback, and support of your strategies?

_____

_____

_____

_____

To execute these actions and steps, what thoughts and emotions would need to be in place in order to support your positive actions?

_____

_____

_____

_____

After executing your new plan/strategy, what results were achieved and what did you learn?

_____

_____

_____

_____

CHAPTER
14

The Final Word

Your success in using the Map of Leadership Maturity™ to help you develop and strengthen your inner-core values, beliefs, thoughts, emotions, and behavioral tendencies as a critical pathway to building and strengthening your outer-core leadership competencies is based on your attitude and mentality. Using The Map as a key element, I have done executive coaching with well over 200 leaders and future leaders across the globe, and I have directly witnessed and experienced its power in helping leaders unlock and unleash their massive potential. The Map contains the important markers and signs that can help guide you to achieving greater maturity and success. However, the most important element in making The Map work is the attitude that you, as a leader or emerging leader, possess toward growing, maturing, and becoming the absolute best you can be.

So what attitude do you need to make The Map work for you?

BE (THE ABSOLUTE BEST OF) YOURSELF

Trying to conform to other peoples' images of you can be challenging, whether those images come from husbands, wives, relatives, friends, colleagues, or bosses. That said, you owe it to yourself to work hard every day—passionately and diligently—to become all that you are capable of becoming. If the images of others are incongruent or not aligned with the true absolute best that you have to offer and you can honestly say that you have done the work that we have detailed in this book, only then should you consider altering your strategy. Maybe it is time to look for another job.

I have worked with countless leaders who have talked about the mounting pressure they experience from having to conform to the expectations of others—new bosses, customers, and greater demands—not to mention the mounting pressure of life at home. Many describe their reality as debilitating and exhausting. The question I pose to them—always—is the question posed in Chapter 1: "Will you see these mounting pressures as an opportunity or potential derailer"? I tell them, as I tell you now, that *if you truly commit to learning more about yourself and becoming the best you can be, while possessing a great attitude, you will discover that all challenges are truly the seeds of opportunity.* It's up to you to take positive action and implement what you have learned in this book.

RESPECT THE PAST, BUT MOVE ON

Repeat what worked well, improve on your mistakes, and move on. If you want to understand why you behaved in certain ways, change your behavior and then compare the differences brought about by the change.

- *Imagine the ideal you. You* is the key word here, not someone else's idea of who you should be. In other words, don't be controlled by the *shoulds*. Use The Map to create a new compelling picture of yourself at the levels of maturity you want to reach.
- *Think, look, and act the part.* If your self-image is a mature, predominant Thinker on the way to becoming a mature, predominant Driver, think of yourself as a mature Thinker. You may not be a mature, predominant Thinker right now, but The Map can help you visualize and execute the characteristics of one.
- *Don't compare yourself to others.* The Map is not a competition. Each trait is different, and each person you work with is unique

in presenting his or her predominant traits, as well the maturity exhibited in all traits. Focus on you, what you do well, and discover what you can do better. Use The Map to help you improve in areas where your behavior isn't what you want it to be.

- *Reward your accomplishments.* How small they may be doesn't matter. Lack of closure and lack of celebration are major causes of stress. So take some time to enjoy what you have done, and treat yourself to something special: dinner, a movie, and extra time with family and friends.
- *Focus on what you can control.* Worrying about anything else will lead to frustration, disappointment, depression, and failure.
- *Be willing to take risks.* Success is not possible without them.
- *Be patient.* You can't overcome all your derailing traits in the time it takes you to identify them and plan what you want to change. But you can *start* to overcome your bad habits in the time it takes you to create the plan.
- *Don't give up.* Setbacks are setbacks; setbacks are not failures.
- *Involve others.* Ask your manager, employees, and other key stakeholders for feedback, guidance, and support on your IDP. Further, as you implement your IDP, continue to ask them for feedback.

Good luck!

APPENDIX

A

Strategic-Tactical Leadership Index™ (STLI)

A Self-Assessment and/or 360-Degree Assessment for:

[Your Name]

STRATEGIC-TACTICAL LEADERSHIP INDEX™ SURVEY

Introduction

Welcome, and thank you for your valued participation in this Strategic-Tactical Leadership Index™ Survey. The purpose of this survey is for you to gain candid and specific information about your leadership effectiveness. Your feedback will be used to provide insight into your interpersonal strengths as well as potential areas for improvement.

This is a valuable and enlightening process for even the most successful professional. Thank you again for your participation.

About the Competencies: Your feedback is requested in nine categories. Please read each description, and circle the rating you believe best describes your colleague. Additionally, please provide comments for each section that present a picture of specific behaviors your colleague exhibits and your reactions to these behaviors.

Competencies Addressed:

1. Critical thinking
2. Decision making
3. Strategic thinking
4. Emotional leadership
5. Communication skills
6. Talent leadership
7. Team leadership
8. Change leadership
9. Drive for results

JohnMattonePartners, Inc.
407-268-5593
www.johnmattonepartners.com
johnmattonepartners@gmail.com

Rating Scale

Use the rating scale below to rate your colleague's effectiveness in each category. If you are using the STLI as a self-assessment, simply rate your own effectiveness.

Description	Rating
Ineffective: Demonstrates incorrect behavior in this area or does not demonstrate this behavior at all.	1
Somewhat effective: Demonstrates this behavior inconsistently and with minimal success.	2
Effective: Demonstrates this behavior with consistency and regular success.	3
Very effective: Demonstrates this behavior with extreme consistency and with extraordinary success.	4
Most effective: Among the best of the best in this area. A model for others.	5
Does not apply to colleague.	N/A

Examples

Motivation: Example 1

My colleague is motivated by:

①	2	3	4	5	N/A

1. Improving the lives of others.

    Comments: John is often seen and heard making rude comments about our customers. One customer actually overheard John say how annoying it was to take care of the customers and that customer left our business promising to tell everyone she knew not to visit our organization again.

Motivation: Example 2

My colleague is motivated by:

1	2	3	4	⑤	N/A

2. Improving the lives of others.

    Comments: Maria is completely dedicated to improving the lives of others. I have seen her on numerous occasions put aside her personal desires to meet the needs of others. I once heard a customer say that Maria spent three hours waiting with her after the offices were closed to go over her personal legal documents at no *extra* charge.

STRATEGIC-TACTICAL LEADERSHIP INDEX™ SURVEY

Section 1: Critical Thinking

My colleague:

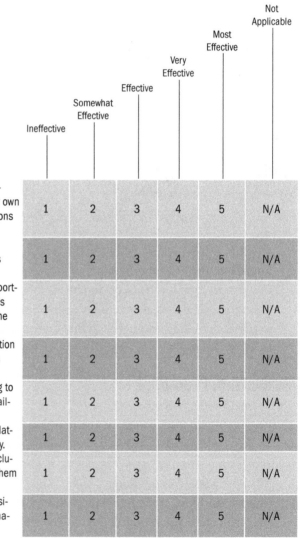

	Ineffective	Somewhat Effective	Effective	Very Effective	Most Effective	Not Applicable
1. Recognizes the important assumptions that underlie their own position as well as the positions advanced by others.	1	2	3	4	5	N/A
2. Analyzes information and positions advanced by others objectively and accurately.	1	2	3	4	5	N/A
3. Questions the validity of supporting evidence and understands how emotion can influence the situation.	1	2	3	4	5	N/A
4. Able to bring diverse information together that logically follows from the available evidence.	1	2	3	4	5	N/A
5. Able to avoid overgeneralizing to other situations based on available evidence.	1	2	3	4	5	N/A
6. Raises vital questions, formulating them clearly and precisely.	1	2	3	4	5	N/A
7. Comes to well-reasoned conclusions and solutions, testing them against relevant standards.	1	2	3	4	5	N/A
8. Ability to adjust their own position based on relevant information and data.	1	2	3	4	5	N/A

Please provide frank and specific feedback concerning this individual's observable behaviors and your reactions to those behaviors.	*Comments:*
	_____
	_____
	_____
	_____

Section 2: Decision Making

My colleague:

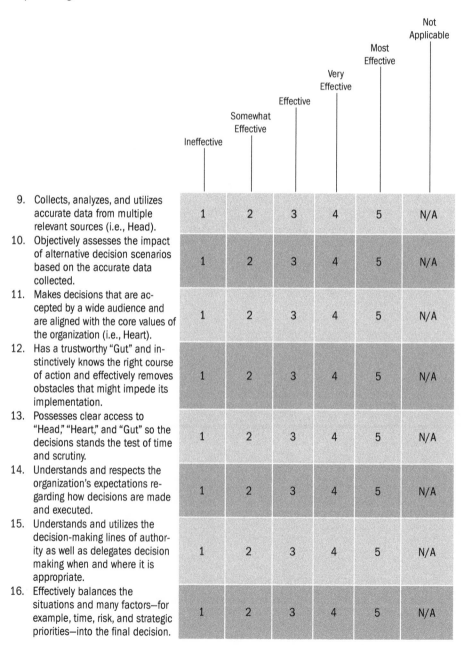

	Ineffective	Somewhat Effective	Effective	Very Effective	Most Effective	Not Applicable
9. Collects, analyzes, and utilizes accurate data from multiple relevant sources (i.e., Head).	1	2	3	4	5	N/A
10. Objectively assesses the impact of alternative decision scenarios based on the accurate data collected.	1	2	3	4	5	N/A
11. Makes decisions that are accepted by a wide audience and are aligned with the core values of the organization (i.e., Heart).	1	2	3	4	5	N/A
12. Has a trustworthy "Gut" and instinctively knows the right course of action and effectively removes obstacles that might impede its implementation.	1	2	3	4	5	N/A
13. Possesses clear access to "Head," "Heart," and "Gut" so the decisions stands the test of time and scrutiny.	1	2	3	4	5	N/A
14. Understands and respects the organization's expectations regarding how decisions are made and executed.	1	2	3	4	5	N/A
15. Understands and utilizes the decision-making lines of authority as well as delegates decision making when and where it is appropriate.	1	2	3	4	5	N/A
16. Effectively balances the situations and many factors—for example, time, risk, and strategic priorities—into the final decision.	1	2	3	4	5	N/A

Please provide frank and specific feedback concerning this individual's observable behaviors and your reactions to those behaviors.

Comments:

_____

_____

_____

_____

Section 3: Strategic Thinking

My colleague:

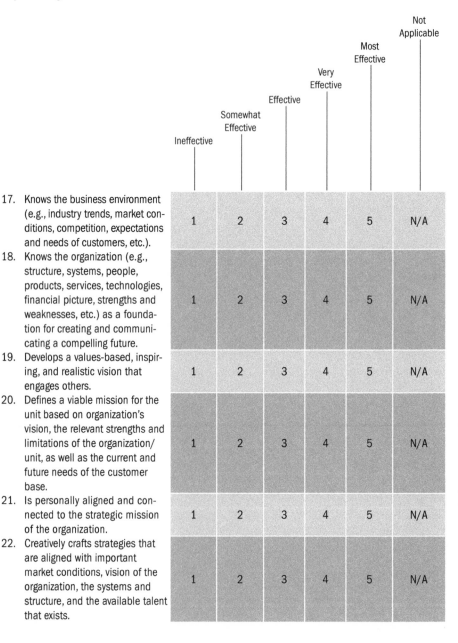

	Ineffective	Somewhat Effective	Effective	Very Effective	Most Effective	Not Applicable
17. Knows the business environment (e.g., industry trends, market conditions, competition, expectations and needs of customers, etc.).	1	2	3	4	5	N/A
18. Knows the organization (e.g., structure, systems, people, products, services, technologies, financial picture, strengths and weaknesses, etc.) as a foundation for creating and communicating a compelling future.	1	2	3	4	5	N/A
19. Develops a values-based, inspiring, and realistic vision that engages others.	1	2	3	4	5	N/A
20. Defines a viable mission for the unit based on organization's vision, the relevant strengths and limitations of the organization/unit, as well as the current and future needs of the customer base.	1	2	3	4	5	N/A
21. Is personally aligned and connected to the strategic mission of the organization.	1	2	3	4	5	N/A
22. Creatively crafts strategies that are aligned with important market conditions, vision of the organization, the systems and structure, and the available talent that exists.	1	2	3	4	5	N/A

23. Effectively translates strategies into goals that are specific, measureable, achievable, realistic, and time limited.

1	2	3	4	5	N/A

24. Uses a measurement philosophy and approach to ensure that goals are accomplished.

1	2	3	4	5	N/A

Please provide frank and specific feedback concerning this individual's observable behaviors and your reactions to those behaviors.

Comments:

_____

_____

_____

_____

Section 4: Emotional Leadership

My colleague:

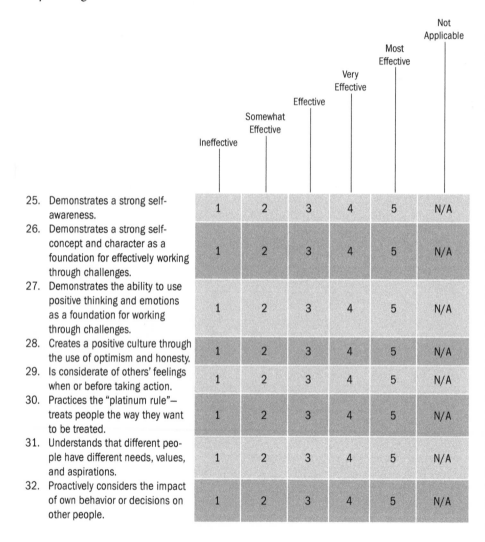

	Ineffective	Somewhat Effective	Effective	Very Effective	Most Effective	Not Applicable
25. Demonstrates a strong self-awareness.	1	2	3	4	5	N/A
26. Demonstrates a strong self-concept and character as a foundation for effectively working through challenges.	1	2	3	4	5	N/A
27. Demonstrates the ability to use positive thinking and emotions as a foundation for working through challenges.	1	2	3	4	5	N/A
28. Creates a positive culture through the use of optimism and honesty.	1	2	3	4	5	N/A
29. Is considerate of others' feelings when or before taking action.	1	2	3	4	5	N/A
30. Practices the "platinum rule"—treats people the way they want to be treated.	1	2	3	4	5	N/A
31. Understands that different people have different needs, values, and aspirations.	1	2	3	4	5	N/A
32. Proactively considers the impact of own behavior or decisions on other people.	1	2	3	4	5	N/A

Please provide frank and specific feedback concerning this individual's observable behaviors and your reactions to those behaviors.	*Comments:*
	_____
	_____
	_____
	_____

Section 5: Communication Skills

My colleague:

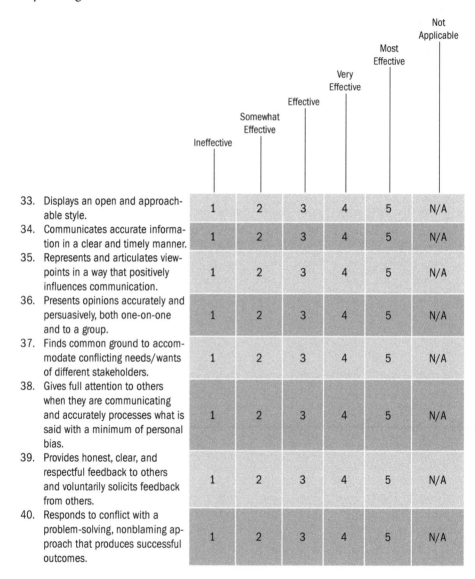

	Ineffective	Somewhat Effective	Effective	Very Effective	Most Effective	Not Applicable
33. Displays an open and approach-able style.	1	2	3	4	5	N/A
34. Communicates accurate informa-tion in a clear and timely manner.	1	2	3	4	5	N/A
35. Represents and articulates view-points in a way that positively influences communication.	1	2	3	4	5	N/A
36. Presents opinions accurately and persuasively, both one-on-one and to a group.	1	2	3	4	5	N/A
37. Finds common ground to accom-modate conflicting needs/wants of different stakeholders.	1	2	3	4	5	N/A
38. Gives full attention to others when they are communicating and accurately processes what is said with a minimum of personal bias.	1	2	3	4	5	N/A
39. Provides honest, clear, and respectful feedback to others and voluntarily solicits feedback from others.	1	2	3	4	5	N/A
40. Responds to conflict with a problem-solving, nonblaming ap-proach that produces successful outcomes.	1	2	3	4	5	N/A

Please provide frank and specific feedback concerning this individual's observable behaviors and your reactions to those behaviors.

Comments:

_____

_____

_____

_____

Section 6: Talent Leadership

In team interactions, my colleague:

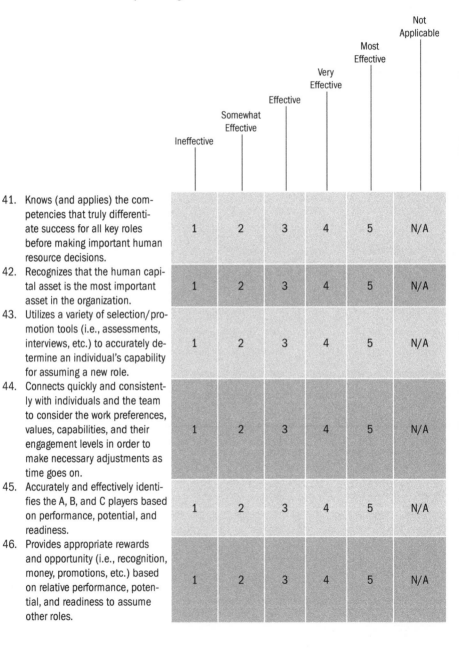

	Ineffective	Somewhat Effective	Effective	Very Effective	Most Effective	Not Applicable
41. Knows (and applies) the competencies that truly differentiate success for all key roles before making important human resource decisions.	1	2	3	4	5	N/A
42. Recognizes that the human capital asset is the most important asset in the organization.	1	2	3	4	5	N/A
43. Utilizes a variety of selection/promotion tools (i.e., assessments, interviews, etc.) to accurately determine an individual's capability for assuming a new role.	1	2	3	4	5	N/A
44. Connects quickly and consistently with individuals and the team to consider the work preferences, values, capabilities, and their engagement levels in order to make necessary adjustments as time goes on.	1	2	3	4	5	N/A
45. Accurately and effectively identifies the A, B, and C players based on performance, potential, and readiness.	1	2	3	4	5	N/A
46. Provides appropriate rewards and opportunity (i.e., recognition, money, promotions, etc.) based on relative performance, potential, and readiness to assume other roles.	1	2	3	4	5	N/A

47. Creates individual development plans that target both the strengths that need to be sustained and the development needs that each individual needs to focus on.

1	2	3	4	5	N/A

48. Provides targeted development (e.g., on-the-job experiences, coaching, and training programs) that enable individuals to become the best they can be.

1	2	3	4	5	N/A

Please provide frank and specific feedback concerning this individual's observable behaviors and your reactions to those behaviors.

Comments:

_____

_____

_____

_____

Section 7: Team Leadership

My colleague:

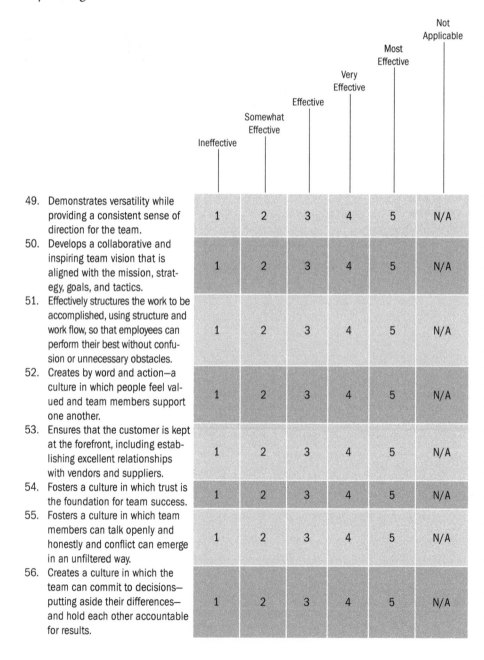

	Ineffective	Somewhat Effective	Effective	Very Effective	Most Effective	Not Applicable
49. Demonstrates versatility while providing a consistent sense of direction for the team.	1	2	3	4	5	N/A
50. Develops a collaborative and inspiring team vision that is aligned with the mission, strategy, goals, and tactics.	1	2	3	4	5	N/A
51. Effectively structures the work to be accomplished, using structure and work flow, so that employees can perform their best without confusion or unnecessary obstacles.	1	2	3	4	5	N/A
52. Creates by word and action—a culture in which people feel valued and team members support one another.	1	2	3	4	5	N/A
53. Ensures that the customer is kept at the forefront, including establishing excellent relationships with vendors and suppliers.	1	2	3	4	5	N/A
54. Fosters a culture in which trust is the foundation for team success.	1	2	3	4	5	N/A
55. Fosters a culture in which team members can talk openly and honestly and conflict can emerge in an unfiltered way.	1	2	3	4	5	N/A
56. Creates a culture in which the team can commit to decisions—putting aside their differences—and hold each other accountable for results.	1	2	3	4	5	N/A

Please provide frank and specific feedback concerning this individual's observable behaviors and your reactions to those behaviors.

Comments:

_____

_____

_____

_____

Section 8: Change Leadership

My colleague:

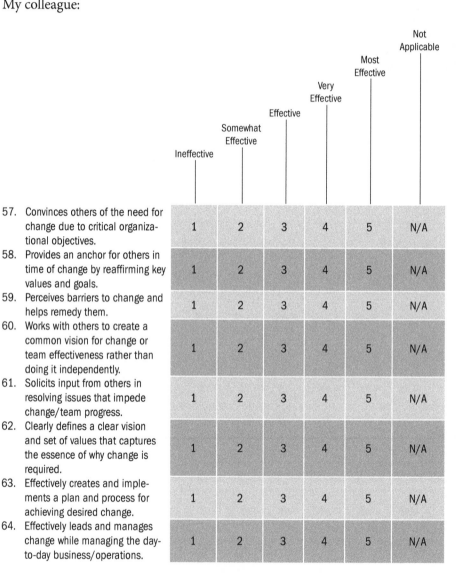

	Ineffective	Somewhat Effective	Effective	Very Effective	Most Effective	Not Applicable
57. Convinces others of the need for change due to critical organizational objectives.	1	2	3	4	5	N/A
58. Provides an anchor for others in time of change by reaffirming key values and goals.	1	2	3	4	5	N/A
59. Perceives barriers to change and helps remedy them.	1	2	3	4	5	N/A
60. Works with others to create a common vision for change or team effectiveness rather than doing it independently.	1	2	3	4	5	N/A
61. Solicits input from others in resolving issues that impede change/team progress.	1	2	3	4	5	N/A
62. Clearly defines a clear vision and set of values that captures the essence of why change is required.	1	2	3	4	5	N/A
63. Effectively creates and implements a plan and process for achieving desired change.	1	2	3	4	5	N/A
64. Effectively leads and manages change while managing the day-to-day business/operations.	1	2	3	4	5	N/A

Please provide frank and specific feedback concerning this individual's observable behaviors and your reactions to those behaviors.

Comments:

_____

_____

_____

_____

Section 9: Drive for Results

My colleague:

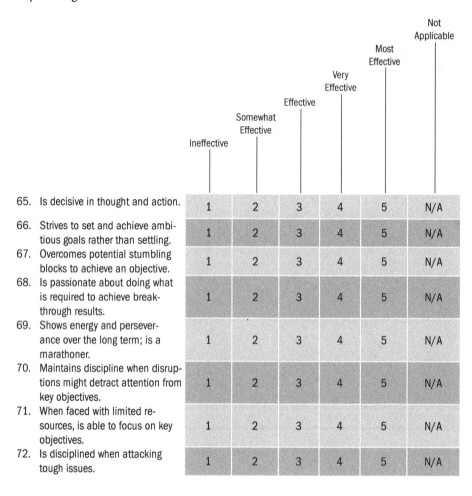

	Ineffective	Somewhat Effective	Effective	Very Effective	Most Effective	Not Applicable
65. Is decisive in thought and action.	1	2	3	4	5	N/A
66. Strives to set and achieve ambitious goals rather than settling.	1	2	3	4	5	N/A
67. Overcomes potential stumbling blocks to achieve an objective.	1	2	3	4	5	N/A
68. Is passionate about doing what is required to achieve breakthrough results.	1	2	3	4	5	N/A
69. Shows energy and perseverance over the long term; is a marathoner.	1	2	3	4	5	N/A
70. Maintains discipline when disruptions might detract attention from key objectives.	1	2	3	4	5	N/A
71. When faced with limited resources, is able to focus on key objectives.	1	2	3	4	5	N/A
72. Is disciplined when attacking tough issues.	1	2	3	4	5	N/A

Please provide frank and specific feedback concerning this individual's observable behaviors and your reactions to those behaviors.	*Comments:*
	_____
	_____
	_____
	_____

APPENDIX

B

The STLI Developmental Strategies

Competency	Skill	Development Strategy
Drive for Results	Setting high standards and motivating others to excel	Emphasize the importance of meeting or exceeding individual and team goals, and how doing so impacts the business. Convey excitement and energy around goals (the more enthusiastic you are about the goals, the more committed others will be to achieving them and supporting you). Create an environment where team members understand that excellent performance is rewarded and often recognized with new opportunities. Expect the best from your people and you're more likely to get it. Research shows that low expectations lead to low performance, even when leaders don't think they're communicating a lack of confidence.

Competency	Skill	Development Strategy
		Look for opportunities to increase team and individual performance expectations over time. Competition and customer expectations are always increasing, and last year's performance level may not be good enough for next year's success.
		Set an example of excellence by the hours you work, the energy you display, and driving for continuous improvement.
		Identify a leader in your company who comes across as being really excellent and who brings out the best in others. Make a list of the specific behaviors that he/she uses, and incorporate some of them into your own style.
		Don't ask team members to do things you aren't willing to do yourself. Personally perform routine tasks occasionally to demonstrate that everyone's work is important and that you are willing to pitch in to help the team succeed.
		Act with commitment, excellence, and integrity in everything you say and do.
		Drive by Dan Pink (Riverhead Trade, 2011).
		True Professionalism: The Courage to Care About Your People, Your Clients and Your Career by David H. Maister (Free Press, 1st Touchstone Ed., 2000).
		The 7 Habits of Highly Effective People by Steven R. Covey (Simon & Schuster, 2005).
		Motivational Management: Inspiring Your People for Maximum Performance by Alexander Hiam (American Management Association, 2002).
		Peak Performers: How to Get the Best from Yourself, Your Coworkers, Your Staff by National Seminars (Career Press, 2001).
		Coaching for Commitment: Interpersonal Strategies for Obtaining Superior Performance from Individuals and Teams by Dennis C. Kinlaw (Pfeiffer, 1999).
Team Leadership	Holding people and teams accountable for achieving results	Define the requirements and performance standards for the products and services your group produces, collectively and for individuals.
		Ensure each employee has clear objectives/expectations and understands the role he/she plays in achieving the team's goals.
		Ask your employees if they will be able to meet their goals; gain their commitment. Recognize/reward individuals when they proactively seek (or at least willingly accept) higher performance goals.

Competency	Skill	Development Strategy
Talent Leadership/ Communication Skills	Providing feedback and coaching to help others develop	If you see performance start to slip below established goals, step in quickly to ensure employees know what the goals are and that they are accountable for achieving them.
		In turbulent times, employees are apt to become preoccupied with issues beyond their performance goals. Keep them focused on their goals, but be sensitive to the concerns they may be dealing with.
		Meet with your team and discuss the best ways to improve the accountability for goals. Remember that ultimately you want to build a culture where everyone on the team holds each other accountable for results, not just you.
		Keeping Employees Accountable for Results: Quick Tips for Busy Managers by Brian Miller (AMACOM, 2006).
		Advantage by Patrick Lencioni (Josey-Bass, 2012).
		The Leadership Challenge, 4th ed. by James M. Kouzes and Barry Z. Posner (Jossey-Bass, 2007).
		Results-Based Leadership by Dave Ulrich et al. (Harvard Business School Press, 1999).
		The Five Dysfunctions of a Team by Patrick Lencioni (Josey-Bass, 2002).
		Provide immediate feedback whenever possible. Focus on specific, concrete behaviors and results. When pointing out an ineffective behavior, describe the correct behavior that should replace it.
		Go out of your way to catch people doing things right, and reinforce those behaviors or results. Don't focus only on the negatives or only managing by exception.
		Create opportunities for more feedback to occur. Set up periodic meetings for your team, and debrief at the end of major projects.
		Rather than merely providing quick solutions to problems yourself, guide others through issues or problems in a way that enables them to solve such problems on their own in the future.
		View your primary role as a leader as being one of helping your team and individual team members be successful, and not just someone who enforces policies. Your success as a leader depends on each of them being successful.
		Encourage your team members to come to you when they have questions or problems, and thank them when they do that, even when you're busy with other matters. Issues and problems that don't get surfaced and resolved just become bigger and eventually impact productivity and quality.

Competency	Skill	Development Strategy
Talent Leadership	Dealing effectively with employee performance problems	Share your knowledge with your team. Teaching others is a good way to further develop your own knowledge and skills. This also encourages the team to utilize you as a teaching resource.
		Powerful Performance Management by John Mattone (AMACOM, 2012).
		Power Mentoring: How Successful Mentors and Protégés Get the Most Out of Their Relationships by Ellen A. Ensher and Susan E. Murphy (Jossey-Bass, 2005).
		Co-Active Coaching: New Skills for Coaching People Toward Success in Work and Life by Laura Whitworth, et al. (Davies-Black Publishing, 2007).
		The One Minute Manager by Kenneth H. Blanchard and Spencer Johnson (William Morrow, 2001).
		Giving Feedback to Subordinates (Center for Creative Leadership) by Raoul J. Buron and Dana McDonald-Mann (Jossey-Bass, 2007).
		Coaching, Mentoring and Managing: Breakthrough Strategies to Solve Performance Problems and Build Winning Teams by Micki Holliday (Career Press, 2001).
		One of the most difficult aspects of being a manager is dealing with performance problems. Don't be timid about asking for advice from your manager, other experienced leaders, or HR. In handling really tough situations, it's often helpful to get input on your plan before you take action.
		Become thoroughly familiar with whatever policies and procedures your company has for handling disciplinary problems, especially with respect to documentation. Check with your HR department if you're unsure. Inconsistency, and not following the proper steps, can lead to serious negative consequences.
		Follow these guidelines when managing a performance issue: (1) Describe specifically what behaviors or results are deficient, and explain why improvement is necessary (e.g., impact on the business); (2) ask the employee for his/her ideas on causes of the problem and how it might be corrected; (3) gain commitment that the agreed-to actions will be taken (ask whether he/she thinks the problem will then get corrected; if the answer isn't a clear yes, then rework the plan); (4) follow up on their performance, and be sure to recognize and reinforce any improvements.

Competency	Skill	Development Strategy
		Confront performance problems early. Leaders tend to delay confronting problems, hoping they'll resolve themselves, but that's not in the best interest of the business or the employee.
		Be honest in giving feedback and don't sugarcoat things. Give people the feedback they need, even when it's difficult.
		When dealing with a performance problem, attack the problem, not the person, and get the employee involved in determining how to resolve the problem.
		Make sure the employee understands that responsibility for correcting a performance problem is in his or her hands, not in yours. But also explain that you will provide support as needed.
		Fails to Meet Expectations: Successful Strategies for Reviewing Underperforming Employees by Corey Sandler and Janice Keefe (Adams Media Corporation, 2007).
		Growing Great Employees: Turning Ordinary People into Extraordinary Performers by Erika Andersen (Portfolio Hardcover, 2006).
		Improving Employee Performance Through Appraisal and Coaching by Donald L. Kirkpatrick (AMACOM, 2005).
		Improving Employee Performance Through Workplace Coaching: A Practical Guide to Performance Management by Earl Carter (Kogan Page, 2005).
		Difficult Conversations by Douglas Stone et al. (Penguin, 2010).
		Crucial Conversations by Kerry Patterson et al. (McGraw-Hill, 2011).
Communication/ Team Leadership/ Emotional Leadership	Dealing with conflict situations.	When you seem to be in a conflict situation, before disagreeing with the other person, restate what you believe to be his/her opinion. Ensure that conflict is not simply a matter of misunderstanding or miscommunication.
		Determine whether a conflict is being caused by differences in goals, competition for resources, failure to communicate, disagreement over standards, or something else. Then deal with the cause of the conflict, not the symptoms.
		Focus on facts and issues, not personalities. Approach conflict situations rationally, not emotionally.
		Encourage your staff to resolve conflicts themselves and not always come to you for resolution (but be ready to step in when it's necessary).

Competency	Skill	Development Strategy
		If the collaboration among groups reporting to you isn't as good as you'd like, meet with the group leaders to see whether a conflict or other issues are causing the problem. As you lead the discussion, get people to focus on the overall goals for your unit and the company.
		Plan your negotiations in advance; understand the position of others, what's important to them, and what's important to you.
		During negotiations with another group, focus on the objectives you have in common and strive for win-win solutions.
		When negotiating, get clear in your own mind in advance what you're willing to give up and what you can't. Make concessions as necessary to achieve outcomes that will be best for the company overall.
		Emotional Intelligence by Daniel Goleman (Bantam, 2005).
		Conflict Management: A Communication Skills Approach by Deborah Borisoff and David A. Victor (Allyn & Bacon, 1997).
		Working Through Conflict: Strategies for Relationships, Groups and Organizations By Joseph P. Folger et al. (Addison Wesley, 1996).
		Mastering Business Negotiation: A Working Guide to Making Deals and Resolving Conflict by Roy J. Lewicki and Alexander Hiam (Jossey-Bass, 2006).
		Negotiating Skills for Managers by Steven Cohen (McGraw-Hill, 2002).
		Seal the Deal: 130 Surefire Negotiating Strategies by Leonard Korn et al. (W. W. Norton, 2004).
Talent Leadership	Identifying and retaining talent	Identify the key talent in your unit, that is, employees who have significant potential to advance and make a greater contribution to the business and employees whose retention is critical. Be sure not to overlook newer, lower-level employees.
		For each high-potential employee, create a fast-track development plan to accelerate their growth. Work with each employee to tailor the plan to their particular needs and career aspirations. Make sure the plans are challenged and developing.

Competency	Skill	Development Strategy
		Be creative in identifying development opportunities—on-the-job growth through increased responsibilities, special assignments or task forces, formal training programs inside and outside the company, assigning a special mentor, and cross-functional job rotations.
		Without making commitments that may not be fulfilled, clearly communicate to high-potential employees that they have a good future with the company. (Don't assume they already know it!)
		Be attentive to the job/company/career satisfaction of all your employees, but particularly for highly talented people whose departure would be a significant loss. If you detect any sign of dissatisfaction, take timely action to address the problem.
		Work closely with HR and actively participate in the talent review process, if your organization has one.
		Be a champion of your people and openly communicate with your manager, management above him/her, and HR about the capabilities of your key people. Don't hold on to talent because you need them in your unit. In the long run, getting your top people promoted will benefit both you and the business.
		Make sure subordinate leaders in your unit are also placing emphasis on nurturing talent in their teams. And you do that by setting goals in this area, following up as you would with any goal, and providing support as needed.
		The Deadly Sins of Employee Retention by Mark Murphy and Andrea Burgio-Murphy (BookSurge Publishing, 2006).
		Love 'Em or Lose 'Em: Getting Good People to Stay by Beverly Kaye and Sharon Jordan-Evans (Berrett-Koehler, 2005).
		Winning the Talent Wars: How to Build a Lean, Flexible, High-Performance Workplace by Bruce Tulgan (W. W. Norton, 2002).
		Talent Leadership: A Proven Method for Identifying and Developing High-Potential Employees by John Mattone (AMACOM, 2012).
		Grow Your Own Leaders: How to Identify, Develop, and Retain Leadership Talent by William C. Byham et al. (Prentice Hall, 2002).

Competency	Skill	Development Strategy
Emotional Leadership/ Talent Leadership	Creating the conditions where employees are challenged and engaged	Look for opportunities to increase your employees' authority and accountability. As their capabilities increase, give them decision-making responsibility in areas for which your approval was formerly required.
		Add new tasks to jobs to widen the variety of skills needed. This will reduce boredom and increase motivation. Look for opportunities to assign tasks to individuals that are out of their typical comfort zone.
		Remember that empowerment means sharing both responsibility and authority. Responsibility without authority isn't fair to employees, and authority without responsibility is dangerous for you.
		Recognize that job enrichment—changing jobs to make them more challenging and satisfying—is a technique that can lead to higher quality work and greater commitment.
		When you do give team members increased responsibility and authority, be sure to follow up and provide support as needed. And be tolerant of mistakes as people try out new skills.
		Focus your feedback and recognition on skills development in addition to performance results. If a team member did just okay on an assignment but learned something new in the process, then that's worthy of your attention.
		Let people know how important they are to your team and to the business, and do so frequently.
		Growing Great Employees: Turning Ordinary People into Extraordinary Performers by Erika Andersen (Portfolio Hardcover, 2006).
		The Enthusiastic Employee: How Companies Profit by Giving Workers What They Want by David Sirota et al. (Wharton School Publishing, 2005).
		The Coaching Revolution: How Visionary Managers Are Using Coaching to Empower People and Unlock Their Full Potential by David Logan and John King (Adams Media Corporation, 2004).
		Strengths-Based Leadership by Tom Rath (Gallup, 2005).
		Zapp!: The Lightning of Empowerment: How to Improve Quality, Productivity, and Employee Satisfaction by William Byham and Jeff Cox (Fawcett Books, 1998).

Competency	Skill	Development Strategy
Strategic Thinking/ Critical Thinking	Setting clear priorities for the unit	Document the unit's goals and priorities and provide a copy to all your employees. Focus on those goals that are most important to the company.
		Update goals and objectives when company priorities change or when the resources you have available change.
		Track progress against the unit's goals on an ongoing basis and initiate corrective action when necessary.
		Prioritize problems in terms of (1) the impact they have on the business and (2) how important it is that they be solved soon.
		Look for opportunities in your unit to eliminate work or tasks that aren't really necessary or adding value.
		Periodically review your priorities with your manager to ensure they are aligned with the company's goals.
		Getting Organized at Work: 24 Lessons for Setting Goals, Establishing Priorities, and Managing Your Time by Kenneth Zeigler (McGraw-Hill, 2008).
		Blue Ocean Strategies by W. Chan Kim and Renee Mauborgne (Harvard Business Review Press, 2005).
		The Innovator's Dilemma by Clayton Christensen (Harper Business, 2000).
		Good to Great by Jim Collins (Harper Business, 2001).
Decision Making/ Critical Thinking	Using financial and quantitative data to make decisions	If you don't know how to interpret basic financial statements (e.g., balance sheet, profit and loss), or if you don't understand basic financial measures (e.g., ROI), then look for a course your company offers or an outside course that you can take to shore up your skills in these areas.
		Work with your manager or someone from the finance department to increase your understanding of the budgeting process and financial statements as they are used in your organization.
		Become an expert in being able to interpret and draw correct conclusions from whatever financial or other quantitative measures are used to measure performance in your area.
		To the extent possible, base your decisions on financial and quantitative data, rather than going with subjective judgments.

Competency	Skill	Development Strategy
		Practice translating financial or other quantitative data into meaningful charts and graphs. This will deepen your understanding of the principles behind all the numbers.
		Look for ways to quantify things that were only treated qualitatively in the past. Even if they're not perfect measures, you'll be able to better track trends over time.
		Judgment in Managerial Decision Making, 6th ed. by Max H. Bazerman (Wiley, 2005).
		Management by Measurement: Designing Key Indicators and Performance Measurement Systems by Fiorenzo Franceschini et al. (Springer, 2007).
		By the Seat of Your Pants: The No-Nonsense Business Management Guide by Tom Gegax and Phil Bolsta (Expert Pub., 2005).
		Practical Financial Management: A Guide for Today's Manager by Dmitri Faguet (Wiley, 2003).
		Even You Can Learn Statistics: A Guide for Everyone Who Has Ever Been Afraid of Statistics by David M. Levine and David F. Stephen (Prentice Hall, 2004).
Critical Thinking	Identifying the underlying causes of problems	Think about these questions when addressing a problem: when it began, who was involved, who wasn't, what makes the problem better/worse, is it recurring, and how often does it occur? Look for trends or common patterns.
		Consider when the problem occurs and, just as important, when it doesn't occur. This can often provide new insight into causes.
		Devote enough time to collecting and analyzing information the next time you are faced with an important decision to make or problem to solve. Decide what you will do based on this information, rather than just relying on your gut feeling.
		Don't fixate on a single solution. Make a list of several possible solutions, and then evaluate the pros and cons of each one.
		On complex problems, collect quantitative data and analyze it in terms of causes. It often happens that only one or two things are causing 90% of the problems.
		Pay special attention to recurring problems. This sometimes indicates that the solution you've tried in the past has treated only the symptoms. Dig deeper to uncover the real causes.
		Dive right into challenging issues. Decide on the minimum amount of information you need in order to make a quality decision, and then move forward.

Competency	Skill	Development Strategy
Emotional Leadership/ Communication	Asserting own ideas and persuading others	*101 Creative Problem Solving Techniques: The Handbook of New Ideas for Business*, rev. ed., by James M. Higgins (New Management Publishing, 2005). *Asking the Right Questions: A Guide to Critical Thinking*, 8th ed., by N. Browne and S. Keeley (Prentice Hall, 2006). *Creative Problem Solving* by Thomas Dombroski (iUniverse, 2000). *Smart Choices: A Practical Guide to Making Better Decisions* by John S. Hammond et al. (Broadway, 2002). *The Art of Original Thinking: The Making of a Thought Leader*, 9th ed., by Jan Phillips (Element Press. 2006). Present your opinions forcefully and directly. Avoid phrases like "Don't you think...?", "It seems to me...", "Maybe I'm wrong, but.... "You can be firm and direct without being abrasive. Organize your persuasive reasoning around only three to five main points, and summarize those points when you've finished. Work to build commitment to what you are proposing. Check on the degree of commitment you have actually achieved. Sometimes people will give nonverbal signals that they agree with you, but, when you ask them, they'll give you a different story. Defend your ideas in a positive manner and don't become defensive. Deal directly with challenges, but focus on the facts and rationale, not on the person challenging you. Become a true expert in your area; learn everything you can. Displaying confidence and self-assurance becomes easier and is more credible when you know more about the subject matter than anyone else. Form a positive mental image of yourself as being competent and successful, and keep this image in mind as you interact with others. Over time, your behaviors will change to match the image and you will display more confidence. Don't be a yes-person. Decide what is right and stand up for it. Don't allow yourself to be swayed by what others would like you to say. Don't be intimidated by the status of higher-level managers (but be respectful). Be careful that displaying modesty (which is a virtue) doesn't come across as being overly humble or lacking in confidence. Great leaders aren't humble in displaying their strengths, but they are modest.

Competency	Skill	Development Strategy
		Influencer by Kerry Patterson et al. (McGraw-Hill, 2008).
		Consensus Through Conversation: How to Achieve High-Commitment Decisions by Larry Dressler (Berrett-Koehler, 2006).
		Crucial Conversations: Tools for Talking When Stakes Are High by Kerry Patterson et al. (McGraw-Hill, 2002).
		The Courageous Messenger: How to Successfully Speak Up at Work by Kathleen D. Ryan et al. (Jossey-Bass, 1996).
		Assertiveness Workbook: How to Express Your Ideas and Stand Up for Yourself at Work and in Relationships by Randy J. Paterson (New Harbinger, 2000).
		How to Get Your Message Across: A Practical Guide to Power Communications by David Lewis (Souvenir Press, 1997).
	Exerting influence with internal/external customers	Fully explain and communicate to your team members your commitment to high standards of customer service. Then model the correct behaviors.
		When appropriate, take personal responsibility to meet commitments made to customers: delivery dates, quality requirements, service levels, and the like.
		Strive hard to do things right for your customers 100% of the time. But, because that's not always possible, be prepared to take extraordinary action when things do go wrong. Make sure everyone on your team is obsessed with doing whatever it takes to address problems any time a customer is dissatisfied.
		Promise customers only what you know your team can deliver. If you can exceed those promises, great; they will be excited, not just satisfied. Always overdeliver, never overpromise.
		When your team makes a mistake, take responsibility and don't blame others. Empathize with the customer and address the problem as soon as possible. Initiate action to prevent the problem from recurring.
		Integrity Service: Treat Your Customers Right, Watch Your Business Grow by Ron Willingham (Free Press, 2005).
		Customer Satisfaction: The Customer Experience Through the Customer's Eyes by Nigel Hill et al. (Cogent, 2007).
		Chocolates on the Pillow Aren't Enough: Reinventing the Customer Experience by Jonathan M. Tisch and Karl Weber (Wiley, 2007).

Competency	Skill	Development Strategy
	Knowing how to get things done in organizations	*Complaint Is a Gift: Using Customer Feedback as a Strategic Tool* by Janelle Barlow and Claus Moller (Berrett-Koehler, 1996).
		25 Management Lessons from the Customer's Side of the Counter by James Donnell (McGraw-Hill, 1996).
		Build political support for your ideas in advance by talking with key opinion leaders. However, also be careful not to alienate people by bypassing them.
		Be aware of your company's cultural norms, and be careful not to violate them unless necessary to move the business forward. Know where the land mines are and don't step on one!
		Expand your network in the organization by going out of your way to get to know people who have influence. Learn as much as you can about their needs and priorities.
		Speak positively about other individuals and groups. Over time, this will build up "credits in your account," and you'll have something to withdraw when you need to.
		Keep your manager fully informed about what's going on in your unit, both the good and the bad. That way, he/she can help navigate through the organization and head off anticipated resistance and problems in advance.
		Where you're confronted with barriers or resistance, look for ways to work around them rather than trying to blast through them.
		Take time to learn the unique role that each department plays in achieving success for your company. Pay special attention to how those departments interrelate and/or rely on one another to accomplish company goals.
		When dealing with complex or detailed situations, force yourself to see the big picture to gain a broader perspective. Even the most complicated issues can usually be boiled down to a few important themes.
		Cover Processes at Work: Managing the Five Hidden Dimensions of Organizational Changes by Robert J. Marshak (Berrett-Koehler, 2006).
		Survival of the Savvy: High-Integrity Political Tactics for Career and Company Success by Rich Brandon and Marty Seldman (Free Press, 2004).
		Political Savvy: Systematic Approaches to Leadership Behind the Scenes, 2nd ed., by Joel R. DeLuca (Evergreen Business Group, 1999).

Competency	Skill	Development Strategy
Team Leadership/ Communication Skills	Fostering collaboration within the unit and with other units	*Leadership in a Diverse and Multicultural Environment: Developing Awareness, Knowledge, and Skills* by Mary L. Connerley and Paul B. Pedersen (Sage, 2005).
		Power, Politics, and Organizational Change: Winning the Turf Game by David A. Buchanan and Richard Badham (Sage, 1999).
		Get your team focused on common goals they share rather than just individual goals. Promote cooperation, rather than competition, among team members and groups. Discourage we-versus-they thinking.
		Timely and accurate communications are critical to fostering collaboration and teamwork. Figure out how much communications you need with people in your unit, and with other departments, and then strive to do even more than that.
		Make it a point to publicly recognize and reinforce collaborative behaviors when you see them, and be a role model yourself.
		One way to encourage teamwork and cooperation is to pitch in and actively help your team when they have difficulties or when a specific deadline or objective has to be met.
		Be a role model for your team by learning as much as you can about other teams/functions in the organization and their needs. Also, look for opportunities to serve on cross-functional teams or task forces.
		Be careful to not make disparaging remarks about other departments or functions in front of your team members. Even a casual, off-handed comment can have a far greater impact than you might realize.
		Involve others in the planning process with your team, particularly people who will be affected by what your team does. Determine the support and resources you will need from other groups and be sure to involve them.
		Use the so-called informal organization as a way of keeping others informed and learning what's going on. Wander around, have coffee with people, ask them questions—that sort of thing. Build a network that will help your team successfully interact with others in the organization.
		Perfect Phrases for Building Strong Teams: Hundreds of Ready-to-Use Phrases for Fostering Collaboration, Encouraging Communication, and Growing a Winning Team by Linda Diamond (McGraw-Hill, 2007).

Competency	Skill	Development Strategy
		How to Make Collaboration Work: Powerful Ways to Build Consensus, Solve Problems, and Make Decisions by David Straus and Thomas C. Layton (Barrett-Koehler, 2002).
		Consensus Through Conversation: How to Achieve High-Commitment Decisions by Larry Dressler (Barrett-Koehler, 2006).
		Breakthrough Networking: Building Relationships That Last, 2nd ed., by Lillian D. Bjorseth (Duoforce Enterprises, 2003).
	Taking charge in tough situations	As a leader, step in when you need to and take charge. Don't shy away from situations just because you don't have total responsibility. Be decisive, and take control when it's appropriate to do so.
		Act quickly (but not recklessly) in crisis situations where timely action is important. Be aware of problems that will only get worse when action is delayed.
		Remember that taking charge doesn't necessarily mean that you're making all the decisions or that you're not getting input from others, but rather that you're in control of the situation and taking responsibility.
		When you present a problem to your manager, don't just describe the situation, but also give him/her your recommendation on what should be done about it.
		Don't let your job description constrain you from identifying additional ways you can help the company. Take initiative to find new ways you can make a difference; don't wait to be told.
		Focus on obtaining results, not just on working longer hours; show a bias for action rather than excessive data collection and analysis.
		Habit 1 Be Proactive: The Habit of Choice (The 7 Habits) Audiobook by Stephen R. Covey (Covey, 2006).
		The 13 Secrets of Power Performance by Roger Dawson (Prentice Hall, 1997).
		The Leadership Challenge 4th ed., by James M. Kouzes and Barry Z. Posner (Jossey-Bass, 2007).
		Results-Based Leadership by Dave Ulrich et al. (Harvard Business School Press, 1999.)
		Essential Managers: Do It Now! by Andy Bruce and Ken Langdon (DK Publishers, 2001).
		Execution by Larry Bossidy and Ram Charan (Crown Business, 2002).

Competency	Skill	Development Strategy
Leading/Managing Change	Initiating change to foster continuous improvement	Challenge the fundamental assumptions and accepted ways of doing things; don't be satisfied with the status quo. Strive for continuous improvement.
		Communicate your vision of and enthusiasm for change so that others can more easily understand and buy into the change.
		Provide strong leadership during change; be confident and assertive; nail down expectations, and raise the bar when appropriate.
		When planning change, ensure that objectives, responsibilities, and timeframes are clearly defined and communicated. Develop transition plans when appropriate.
		When you find something that is not working well, take personal responsibility for seeing that it gets fixed. Look for areas where you can eliminate or modify ineffective procedures and systems by creating new approaches.
		When you evaluate opportunities for improvement, pick the changes that will have the biggest impact on the business, but don't overlook making a series of small changes that, in sum, may have just as big an impact. And go after those changes that can really be implemented within a reasonable timeframe.
		Set aside time during team meetings to discuss changes and improvements to your team's work processes and procedures. Encourage team members to be forward thinking and to challenge processes they feel may have become outdated.
		Leadership Agility: Five Levels of Mastery for Anticipating and Initiating Change by William B. Joiner and Stephen A. Josephs (Jossey-Bass, 2006).
		Leading in a Culture of Change by Michael Fullan (Jossey-Bass, 2007).
		Leading Out Loud: Inspiring Change Through Authentic Communications, new and rev. ed., by Terry Pearce (Jossey-Bass, 2003).
		Switch by Chip and Dan Heath (Crown Business, 2010).
		Quality and Process Improvement by Mark Fryman (Cengage-Delmar Learning, 2001).

Competency	Skill	Development Strategy
	Helping employees manage change	Meet with your team to explain the rationale for the change, the potential benefits, and implementation plans. Get their input and gain their support for the change.
		Communicate frequently, accurately, honestly, and completely throughout the change process, particularly about the reasons for change. The research consistently shows that if managers had it to do over again, they would have communicated a lot more.
		Get your team involved in the change process early on; try to stay ahead of the change rather than playing catch-up. Create opportunities for people to provide feedback and share their concerns when changes are implemented.
		Express confidence and optimism that planned changes will result in positive outcomes, and do so repeatedly.
		Once final decisions on a change have been made, concentrate on how to make the change work; don't get stuck in the past.
		Throughout the change process, touch base with your team, your peers, and other appropriate groups regarding the status of the change. Reinforce the positives, and take action to address any problem areas.
		Remember, even well-planned changes are rarely implemented with 100% success. Identify problem areas, and look for opportunities to refine systems and processes over time.
		Change Management Masterclass: A Step-by-Step Guide to Successful Change Management by Mike Green (Kogan Page, 2007).
		Change Basics by Jeffrey Russell (ASTD Press, 2006).
		Making Change Stick: Twelve Principles for Transforming Organizations by Richard C. Reale (Positive Impact Associates, 2005).
		Taking Charge of Change: 10 Principles for Managing People and Performance by Douglas K. Smith (Perseus Publishing, 1997).
		Making Sense of Change Management: A Complete Guide to the Models, Tools & Techniques of Organizational Change by Esther Cameron and Mike Green (Kogan Page, 2004).

APPENDIX

C

The Mattone Leadership Enneagram Index (MLEI)

The Mattone Leadership Enneagram Index (MLEI) is for indentifying predominant leadership styles as well as levels of executive maturity in the individuals you are coaching.

INSTRUCTIONS FOR THOSE TAKING THE MLEI

The MLEI will take 20 minutes to complete. Each statement in the MLEI corresponds to one of the Enneagram's nine leadership personality types. Your task is to record your response (1, 2, 3, 4, or 5; see the following scale) on the line following each statement.

    1 = Strongly disagree with statement

    2 = Disagree with statement

3 = Partially agree/disagree with statement
4 = Agree with statement
5 = Strongly agree with statement

THE HELPER (TWO)

1. I prefer working to help people on a one-to-one basis as opposed to a team basis.
2. I don't like to admit it, but I get into other people's business more than I should.
3. I think I am more people oriented than goal oriented.
4. A lot of thankless tasks seem to fall on my shoulders; I wish others would think of me for a change.
5. I am less disciplined; I know how to be spontaneous and improvise.
6. I am often not sure whether the respect people have for me is sincere or they respect me just because I am nice to them.
7. I spend time with the interpersonal and emotional (as opposed to abstract and mental) aspects of the people and situations I encounter.
8. I am disappointed when I am not repaid for the good things I have done for others.
9. I often get attached to people.
10. I often feel victimized and used by others.
11. I often sense what's going on inside others before they say it out loud.
12. I hate to admit it, but I have a tendency to want to make others feel guilty.

THE ENTERTAINER (THREE)

1. I am described as diplomatic, charming, and ambitious.
2. I think I am more goal oriented than people oriented.
3. I am ambitious and push myself to realize my dreams.
4. It's important to me to let others know how I feel, although I may express myself indirectly.
5. I know how to motivate people and awaken their enthusiasm.
6. I enjoy getting attention from others and being in the limelight.
7. I am very competitive.
8. When I get angry, I can get distant and icy.
9. It's important to me to make favorable impressions.

10. I enjoy talking about myself and being the center of attention.
11. I am optimistic, enthusiastic, and authentic.
12. For the sake of my career, I am prepared to neglect my family and friends.

THE ARTIST (FOUR)

1. One of my greatest assets that I bring to the workplace is the depth of my feelings.
2. It's important to me to let others know how I feel, although I may express myself indirectly.
3. I don't mind revealing my weaknesses to my team, my managers, and others; in fact, I often do.
4. I have the feeling that I will never be fulfilled.
5. I see my life at work as a drama; I am an actor and spectator at the same time.
6. I feel uneasy talking about myself and being the center of attention.
7. I am introspective; I have strong self-awareness.
8. I feel uncomfortable when people depend on me a lot.
9. I am tactful and respectful in my dealings with others.
10. I sometimes hold myself back too much and block doing good things for myself.
11. I have a desire to be an actor, poet, writer, or singer.
12. Down deep, I don't feel at home anywhere.

THE THINKER (FIVE)

1. One of my greatest assets is the sharpness of my mind.
2. I tend not to be motivated by what is socially acceptable.
3. People come to me because I have the knowledge they need.
4. I need study time or at least my own corner to withdraw to when things get stressful.
5. It's important for me to see things as objectively as possible.
6. I like to be alone.
7. I will hesitate to act until I have thought things through carefully.
8. I distrust authority and ignore rules quite often.
9. I prefer structured environments, but I am able to be innovative and unconventional.
10. People say I am argumentative—that I enjoy a good debate.

11. I am a strong systems thinker; I can connect the dots.
12. I often don't put my good ideas on paper, and projects that I have in my head often stay in the planning stages.

THE DISCIPLE (SIX)

1. I prefer working with others in a team effort.
2. I can be stubborn and defensive.
3. I am practical and down-to-earth.
4. I tend to procrastinate.
5. I am well disciplined and organized, and I follow through on details.
6. It makes me furious when others don't follow policies and procedures, and they think they can get away with it.
7. For me, it's important to be proactive about the future so that I'll be better prepared to handle whatever comes my way.
8. It's difficult for me to contain myself when others don't do what they are supposed to do and they put me under pressure.
9. I know that the best results happen when I involve others; I value the input and opinions of others.
10. One of my biggest fears is being taken advantage of.
11. I see myself as a regular/traditional kind of leader.
12. I often have difficulty making decisions, and I find that pressure will often force me to make decisions.

THE ACTIVIST (SEVEN)

1. I am a leader of change.
2. People see me as fast paced, maybe too fast paced.
3. I am challenged by the new, unique, and different.
4. I can easily and quickly get frustrated with everything—myself, others, and events.
5. There is a little bit of a storyteller and entertainer in me.
6. I put down others who can't keep up with me.
7. When my job gives me lemons, I make lemonade.
8. I can be impulsive, outspoken, and exhibit little self-control.
9. I am multitalented; I see myself as a renaissance person with an eye toward the future.
10. When relationships and projects get boring, I tend to abandon them.

11. It's important to me that something is always "going on."
12. I can get offensive toward others in order to get what I want.

THE DRIVER (EIGHT)

1. I act quickly and decisively when things have gone awry.
2. One of my biggest fears is being dependent on anyone else.
3. I am like a rock, steady and sure.
4. Winning is critical to me in everything that I do.
5. I am able to influence others through my confidence and strength of my personality.
6. I like to call all the shots at work.
7. I have always been concerned about justice and what is right at work.
8. When I get angry, I tend to tell people off.
9. I like to negotiate.
10. I don't care if others like me as long as they respect me.
11. I am a resourceful self-starter who brings passion and energy.
12. I don't ever reveal my weaknesses to others.

THE ARBITRATOR (NINE)

1. People confide in me because I make them feel safe and appreciated.
2. It's not always important to tell people how I feel.
3. I am an optimist.
4. I don't always handle pressure well, and I work best at my own pace.
5. I value having a positive, productive work environment.
6. I realize I sometimes avoid thinking about my problems.
7. I am a good listener.
8. I don't like to admit it, but I sometimes let little problems go until they become big problems.
9. I am good at bringing diverse people and groups together to work out issues and move forward.
10. I fear having conflicts with others.
11. I have a great sense of gratitude for what I have in my life.
12. I tend to think that if I let problems run their course, they will eventually evaporate.

THE PERFECTIONIST (ONE)

1. I am formal, direct, and mature.
2. I am often under time pressure.
3. I persuade others with my honesty and reasonableness of my arguments.
4. In my thoughts, I often criticize myself.
5. I am a teacher and coach.
6. I often feel physical tension—in my back, shoulders, and elsewhere.
7. I am disciplined, organized, and meticulous.
8. Others often feel criticized by me.
9. I am wise and discerning; I can evaluate options quickly and make accurate decisions.
10. I enjoy proving others wrong.
11. I am tolerant of my own and others' shortcomings.
12. I can be ruthless and relentless in making sure I am correct.

PLOTTING YOUR MLEI RESULTS

- For each type, total your scores for the 12 items. The maximum score you can achieve is 60.
- Transfer your total scores for each type to the MLEI Profile (Exhibit C.1), and plot your total scores for each type. You can now connect the dots to reveal your predominant type and distinct profile.
- For each type, there is a maturity and derailer score. You can determine your maturity score by summing your scores across all odd items (i.e., 1, 3, 5, 7, 9, 11) and your derailer score by summing all even items (i.e., 2, 4, 6, 8, 10, 12).
- For each type, transfer these results to the MLEI Profile by plotting your maturity and derailer scores for each type. You can now connect the dots to reveal your distinct profile.
- Follow the instructions identified on the MLEI Profile to calculate your Maturity Ratio (MR) for each type.
- Your MR will range from +0.8 to –0.8. If your MR is:

  +0.8 to + 0.4   You are exhibiting very mature attitudes and behaviors associated with that type.

  +0.3 to + 0.39   You are exhibiting high average leadership maturity attitudes and behaviors associated with that type.

EXHIBIT C.1:   **MLEI PROFILE**

	Heart Leaders			Head Leaders			Gut Leaders		
	2 Helper	3 Entertainer	4 Artist	5 Thinker	6 Disciple	7 Activist	8 Driver	9 Arbitrator	1 Perfectionist
Total 60 50 40 30 20 10									
Mature 30 20 10									
Derailer 30 20 10									
Total Score									
MR									
AMR=									

Calculating your maturity ratio (MR):

1. Total maturity score ÷ Total possible maturity score (30)

2. Total derailer score ÷ Total possible derailer score (30)

3. MR = 1−2

Calculating your average maturity ratio (AMR):

1. Sum all nine MR scores ÷ 9 = AMR

Interpretation

+ .4 to + .8 = High executive maturity

+ .3 to + .39 = High average executive maturity

+ .2 to + .29 = Average executive maturity

+ .1 to + .19 = Low average executive maturity

0 to + .09 = Derailer traits are present

Less than 0 = Derailer traits are a concern

+.0.20 to + 0.29	You are exhibiting average leadership maturity associated with that type.
+.0.10 to + 0.19	You are exhibiting low-average leadership maturity associated with that type.
0 to + 0.09	You are exhibiting derailer traits that are potentially limiting your leadership potential and success.
Less than 0	You are exhibiting significant derailer traits that are limiting your leadership potential and success.

- An additional element to examine is to determine the number of types that have pluses (+). Having at least eight out of the nine types with a plus (+) would suggest that you are being consistent across the types. For example, an average MR of +0.20 and eight pluses would mean that you are consistently exhibiting average maturity across the nine types that define your leadership style. As another example, having an average MR of over +0.30 with fewer than eight pluses would suggest you are mature in some of the types and immature in others.

INTERPRETATION OF THE MLEI

Each of the MLEI types embodies a wide range of leader thought and belief patterns, values, attitudes, and behavioral tendencies. In combination, the nine types symbolize the universe of leadership potential that exists in any one individual. One reason we are all similar is that all nine types operate in each of us. One reason we are all different, however, is that their proportion and balance (i.e., degree of maturity or immaturity) are different and constantly shifting.

The nine types of the *Map of Leadership Maturity* reveal the full range of your leadership assets and liabilities. The relative *balance*, however, of a leader's type (as indicated by maturity ratios) produces their distinctive psychological fingerprint. Although their predominant type (i.e., highest score combining both mature and derailer scores) is most revealing and should remain relatively constant, it is the degree of overall development of each of their other types (as well as the associated balance or maturity of all nine types) that changes and evolves.

Your objectives as a leader or emerging leader are to (1) optimize the mature elements of your predominant trait and (2) create development goals and strategies that enable you to grow and mature in each of the other eight traits that comprise their unique leadership fingerprint.

Furthermore, equally important to discovering your most evidenced traits (or highest scores) is to identify the traits that are not evidenced enough. The highest-scoring traits represent areas of leadership potential that you have already activated, whereas the lowest-scoring types represent areas you may need to bring out, but only in a mature fashion.

Heart Leaders: Maturity and Derailer Characteristics

- *Type Two: The Helper:* The functions of *empathy* and *altruism* and the potential for other-directedness, thoughtfulness for others, genuine self-sacrifice, generosity, and nurturance. Negatively, the potential for intrusiveness, possessiveness, manipulation, and self-deception.
- *Type Three: The Entertainer:* The functions of *self-esteem* and *self-development* and the potential for ambition, self-improvement, personal excellence, professional competence, self-assurance, and social self-distinction. Negatively, the potential for pragmatic calculation, arrogant narcissism, the exploitation of others, and hostility.
- *Type Four: The Artist:* The functions of *self-awareness* and *artistic creativity* and the potential for intuition, sensitivity, individualism, self-expression, and self-revelation. Negatively, the potential for self-absorption, self-consciousness, self-doubt, self-inhibition, and depression.

Head Leaders: Maturity and Derailer Characteristics

- *Type Five: The Thinker:* The functions of *mental focus* and *expert knowledge* and the potential for curiosity, perceptiveness, the acquisition of knowledge, inventive originality, and technical expertise. Negatively, the potential for speculative theorizing, emotional detachment, eccentricity, social isolation, and mental projections.
- *Type Six: The Disciple:* The functions of *trust* and *perseverance* and the potential for emotional bonding with others, group identification, sociability, industriousness, loyalty to others, and commitment to larger efforts. Negatively, the potential for dependency, ambivalence, rebelliousness, anxiety, and inferiority feelings.
- *Type Seven: The Activist:* The functions of *spontaneity* and *diverse activity* and the potential for enthusiasm, productivity, achievement, skill acquisition, and the desire for change and variety. Negatively,

the potential for hyperactivity, superficiality, impulsiveness, excessiveness, and escapism.

Gut Leaders: Maturity and Derailer Characteristics

- *Type Eight: The Driver:* The functions of *self-assertion* and *leadership* and the potential for self-confidence, self-determination, self-reliance, magnanimity, and the ability to take personal initiative. Negatively, the potential for domination of others, crude insensitivity, combativeness, and ruthlessness.
- *Type Nine: The Arbitrator:* The functions of *receptivity* and *interpersonal mediation* and the potential for emotional stability, acceptance, unself-consciousness, emotional and physical endurance, and creating harmony with others. Negatively, the potential for passivity, disengaged emotions and attention, neglectfulness, and mental dissociation.
- *Type One: The Perfectionist:* The functions of *ethical standards* and *responsibility* and the potential for moderation, conscience, maturity, self-discipline, and delayed gratification. Negatively, the potential for rigid self-control, impersonal perfectionism, judgmentalism, and self-righteousness.

Fluctuating Scores

If you take the MLEI several times, your predominant trait should remain the same, although you will probably find that the scores for your other traits (as well as their maturity ratios for all nine types) will rise or fall depending on other influences going on at work and at home. A leader having problems with a boss, for instance, is likely to register higher or lower scores in types associated with concerns about relationships, such as Two, Six, and Nine.

Likewise, someone who has been putting a lot of time and energy into work or is having career problems is likely to produce elevated scores in types Three, Eight, and One. After the troubled relationship or the career issues have been resolved (one way or another), the profile for that person may change yet again. The scores for the person's basic personality type may also be affected, although the type itself will remain the same.

APPENDIX

D

The Assessment-Driven Leadership Individual Development Plan

Prepared for: John Smith
ABC Corporation
February 1, 2011

CONTENTS

THE SIX-STEP PROCESS

STEP 1:
Analysis of Your Job
(review Map of Success or relevant competency model)

STEP 2:
Review of Perception-Based Assessments
(360s, Self, and Reviews)

STEP 3:
Review of Objective-Based Assessments

STEP 4:
Data Integration—Intrapersonal, Interpersonal,
Skills, Competencies

STEP 5:
Data Integration Summary—3×3×3×3

STEP 6:
Development Planning

STEP 1: ANALYSIS OF YOUR JOB

The starting point in building your Individual Development Plan (IDP) is to identify the critical strategic competencies, tactical skills, interpersonal skills, and intrapersonal attributes required for success in your role as a leader. Review the Map of Success and/or other leadership competency model, and spend a few minutes thinking about your role and the critical factors that determine success.

In the space below, write down the strategic competencies (e.g., Critical Thinking), tactical leadership skills (e.g., Talent Leadership), interpersonal skills (e.g., Extroversion), and intrapersonal skills (e.g., Self-Awareness) required for success in your role as a leader. Once you have them listed, describe in your own words what you think is the absolute most important requirement for each area.

Domain	Competencies/ Skills	Most Important? Why?
Competencies and Skills Examples: • Decision Making • Change Leadership • Emotional Leadership • Strategic Thinking • Critical Thinking • Talent Leadership • Team Leadership • Drive for Results • Communication Skills		

Interpersonal Attributes
 	
Examples:
 	
• Interpersonal Skill
  – Sociability
  – Amicability
• Understanding Others
  – Empathy
  – Insightfulness
• Creativity
  – Creative Temperament
  – Independence
• Handling Sensitive Problems
  – Dominance
  – Empathy
• Action Orientation
  – Flexibility
  – Sensitivity
• Influence
  – Sociability
  – Dominance
• Extroversion vs. Introversion
• Sensing vs. Intuition
• Thinking vs. Feeling
• Judging vs. Perceiving
• Etc.		

Domain	Competencies/ Skills	Most Important? Why?

Intrapersonal Attributes
 	
Examples
• Self-Awareness
   – Self-Acceptance
   – Empathy
• Self-Control
   – Social Conformity
   – Self-Control
• Resilience
   – Self-Acceptance
   – Well-Being
• Self-Confidence
   – Independence
   – Leadership Potential
• "Leadership Map of Maturity"
  Types and Maturity Levels		

Step 2: Review of Perception-Based Assessments

Multirater assessment data is critically important to understanding *what* you do and *how* you do it on the job. If you have multirater feedback such as 360 assessment results, you can use this section to summarize your results. With 360 data, you should put more weight on how others (i.e., your manager, peers, and direct reports) perceive you than on your own self-ratings. However, in the absence of 360 results, you should use your most recent performance review results, again placing more weight on your manager's perception of your strengths/development opportunities. Review your multirater and/or performance review information and think about what the results reveal about your strengths and opportunities for development in each area. Note your strengths and opportunities in the space provided, and write down the specific multirater item or statement that was most important in leading you to your conclusion.

Domain	Strengths/ Opportunities	Multirater Items/ Examples
Strategic Competencies and Tactical Skills	Strengths: Opportunities:	

Domain	Strengths/ Opportunities	Multirater Items/ Examples
Interpersonal Attributes	Strengths: Opportunities:	
Intrapersonal Attributes	Strengths: Opportunities:	

Step 3: Review of Objective-Based Assessments

Objective-based assessments that measure your inner-core attributes—such as your self-concept, values, beliefs, predominant thinking and emotional patterns, and behavioral interpersonal tendencies—are all designed to help you understand *why* you do what you do. Your inner-core attributes (i.e., intrapersonal) are at the foundation of being able to predict how you behave and the skills and competencies you execute. Your inner-core attributes are typically enduring in that they have been developed, shaped, and reinforced, making them also challenging to change. Some objective assessments—such as skill-based simulations (e.g., TALENTSIM)—don't measure inner-core attributes, but they do measure an individual's performance potential to be able to execute the required skills and competencies that are associated with success in a leadership role. You should incorporate your MLEI Results here in the Intrapersonal section.

Domain	Strengths	Opportunities
Strategic Competencies and Tactical Skills		

Domain	Strengths	Opportunities
Interpersonal Attributes		
Intrapersonal Attributes		

STEP 4: DATA INTEGRATION—INTRAPERSONAL

It is now important to compare and contrast your objective assessment results with whatever perception-based assessments you have utilized—across all three areas of defined leadership success: Intrapersonal, Interpersonal, and Tactical/ Strategic Competencies. It is important to note that most 360 assessments are not focused on measuring intrapersonal attributes; sometimes, however, raters are asked to evaluate behaviors that reflect inner-core attributes such as self-awareness or self-image. Please recognize that such attributes cannot be observed directly by others; they are inferred, based on the behaviors exhibited. Therefore, as you complete the matrix you might find that you are utilizing your own self-perceptions to define the horizontal axis of the matrix—which is fine. When you start completing the matrices for the Interpersonal attributes and Skills/Competencies, it will be more appropriate to utilize your 360 assessment results (in terms of how others see you) and/or your performance review feedback results to populate the horizontal axis.

Each matrix combines two axes: Objective Assessment Results (vertical) and Perception Assessment Results (horizontal). The result is four distinct quadrants:

- *Indisputable Strengths (IS):* Objective assessment results reveal strengths that confirm perceptions (++)
- *Surprise Strengths (SS):* Objective assessment results reveal strengths that are discrepant with perceptions (+-)
- *Indisputable Development Opportunities (IDO):* Objective assessment results reveal development opportunities that confirm perceptions (--)
- *Surprise Development Opportunities (SDO):* Objective assessment results reveal development opportunities that are discrepant with perceptions (-+)

Ultimately, the strength of your IDP will be in direct proportion to identifying with the help of your coach and key stakeholders two or three goals and action plans for each quadrant but more emphasis on the discrepant quadrants (SS & SDO) because most leaders find it empowering to be able to leverage underused talents and deal with the blind spots that are revealed in the SDO quadrant.

Intrapersonal Matrix

PERCEPTION

	+	−
+	Indisputable Strength (IS)	Surprise Strength (SS)
−	Surprise Development Needs (SDN)	Indisputable Development Needs (IDN)

OBJECTIVE

Interpersonal Matrix

PERCEPTION

	+	−
	Indisputable Strength (IS)	**Surprise Strength (SS)**
+		
	Surprise Development Needs (SDN)	**Indisputable Development Needs (IDN)**
−		

OBJECTIVE

Skills/Competencies Matrix

PERCEPTION

	+	−
	Indisputable Strength (IS)	**Surprise Strength (SS)**
+		
	Surprise Development Needs (SDN)	**Indisputable Development Needs (IDN)**
−		

OBJECTIVE

STEP 5: DATA INTEGRATION (3×3×3×3)

In the following three matrices, carry over the two strengths and development opportunities that you believe are the most important to your success. If necessary, go back and review your work at Step 1 to help you align what is important with what is required for success in your role. After you have identified two for each quadrant, now eliminate one. That will leave you with one strength or development opportunity per quadrant and your summary matrix will contain no more than three per quadrant, hence the 3×3×3×3.

Intrapersonal

Indisputable Strength (IS)	Surprise Strength (SS)
Surprise Development Needs (SDN)	Indisputable Development Needs (IDN)

Interpersonal

Indisputable Strength (IS)	Surprise Strength (SS)
Surprise Development Needs (SDN)	Indisputable Development Needs (IDN)

Competencies/Skills

Indisputable Strength (IS)	Surprise Strength (SS)
Surprise Development Needs (SDN)	Indisputable Development Needs (IDN)

Summary Matrix—3×3×3×3

Indisputable Strength (IS)	Surprise Strength (SS)
Surprise Development Needs (SDN)	Indisputable Development Needs (IDN)

STEP 6: INDIVIDUAL DEVELOPMENT PLAN

SS Goals/Why	Development Actions/ Support Needed	Results		
		3 months	6 months	9 months
SDN Goals/WHY				
IS Goals/WHY				
IDN Goals/WHY				

APPENDIX

E

Sample Leadership Individual Development Plan

CREATING THE INDIVIDUAL DEVELOPMENT PLAN

An Effective Plan

This plan is a summary of your strengths, career directions, and areas on which your development will focus.

Effective development plans are:

- Relevant to your organization's needs.
- Based on an objective, accurate assessment of strengths and needs.
- Focused on challenging development activities targeted to sustaining/

219

strengthening your strengths as well as focusing on addressing your development needs.

- Inclusive and tap others for coaching and feedback on progress.
- Driven by you. You own the plan and implement it; it is best seen as a journey, not a destination.

Building the Plan

- *Indisputable Strengths:* These are your towering strengths, abilities that come quickly to mind when people think about what it is you bring to the organization.
- *Surprise Strengths:* Identify one or two based on the assessment results and your discussion with your coach.
- *Development needs:* The key areas on which you need to focus development. These include your *indisputable* and *surprise* development needs. To be practical, limit these to one or two per area; they should be related to making you the best in your current role and positioning yourself for whatever future opportunities may develop for you.
- *Development objectives and actions (see Step 6 in Assessment-Driven IDP Tool):*

Development objectives describe your areas for development.

- Limit your developmental objectives to one or two.
- Focus on changes in knowledge, skills, or behaviors.

Action steps provide experiences and practice needed to develop. Steps might include:

- Further clarification or feedback.
- Actions to be taken within your present job assignment.
- Additional responsibilities or reassignments.
- Coaching and training.
- Progress reviews with your boss or others at regular intervals.

You will benefit most from action steps that:

- Place you outside your comfort zone.
- Provide a diversity of experiences that will broaden your skills and perspectives.
- Improve awareness of your impact on others.
- Give practice needed to perform new skills even under stress.
- Include assignments where either success or failure is possible.

Include in your plan ways to measure your progress. This should include regular reviews of your plan with your boss, your coach, or any other appropriate people.

STRENGTHS

- *Strategic Thinking:* Able to create strategies and plans to achieve business objectives. Understand the big picture and all the forces at work.
- *Critical Thinking:* Apply disciplined market and competitor analysis to identify sales opportunities and focus efforts for maximum impact.
- *Team Leadership:* Understand and communicate the vision and business objectives to the team. Motivate others to make sales and achieve business objectives.

CAREER DIRECTIONS

These goals are based on present circumstances and are open to modification.

- Next 1–2 years: Demonstrate value and success as Sales Manager.
- Next 3–5 years: Advance to Vice President of Sales and Marketing.
- Long-term, 5+ years: Advance to President.

DEVELOPMENT NEEDS

- Improve individual performance management skills so that I can better manage my sales force.
- Expand working relationships with peers.
- Strengthen creative thinking.

DEVELOPMENT OBJECTIVES

Development Objective 1

Build a high-performance work environment for my sales team that fosters accountability, creativity, and professional growth.

Action Steps:

- Transform current job descriptions and department goals into a performance management system that ties individual responsibilities, actions, and results to measurable business objectives. Consult boss and HR group regarding this action step. (End of Q1)

- Establish one-on-one meetings at least monthly that enable direct reports to evaluate progress, seek insights and feedback, and adjust activities. (End of Q1)
- Hold biweekly team meetings to encourage knowledge sharing and common understanding of progress against objectives. Also use these meetings to have fun and foster creativity; do brainstorming, use mind-bender exercises to get us thinking out of the box. (End of Q1)
- Work with direct reports to create individual development plans utilizing HR organization and tools (like this template). (End of Q2)
- Talk with HR department about training programs, either in-house or out, that will help me take performance management to the next level. (End of Q4)

Development Objective 2

Broaden my in-house network while adding value to the company (so that this is not just a social exercise).

Action Steps:

- Work more closely with Rob and his organization. Ask Rob to assign me to a specific project within his organization where my marketing skills compliment the production team. (End of Q2)
- Serve on a regional cross-functional committee over the next year. Ask Frank for an appointment ASAP.
- Expand network through two informal lunches per month with members from different functional organizations to learn new approaches to business opportunities.

Development Objective 3

Strengthen creative thinking skills to make decisions without complete reliance on data.

Action Steps:

- Develop a consulting relationship with Glenn to learn how he thinks about business opportunities. Get into his head about how he thinks about making decisions and how he uses his instincts. (This ties in with the networking lunches above.)

- Attend this year's industry conference and have a veteran provide a tour and overview. Identify top products and what makes them number one. Write a one-page summary of findings, including implications for either my group or the company as a whole. Review this with my boss and at least two other people.

Progress Review

Review plan quarterly with one-on-one meetings with boss.

INDEX

ABOUT THE AUTHOR

John Mattone is widely regarded as the world's leading authority on the Future Trends of Leadership Development & Talent Management. In 2011, he was named by the prestigious *Thinkers50* as one of the fastest rising stars in the field of leadership development. Recently, he was named by *Leadership Excellence Magazine* as one of the world's top leadership consultants, speakers, and coaches.

John Mattone is recognized globally as an inspiring keynote speaker, prolific author, and highly sought-after executive coach. John is the President of JohnMattonePartners (JMP), a global leadership consulting firm that specializes in executive assessment, development, and coaching. John has over 30 years of experience in the fields of executive development and human capital management as an entrepreneur who has built two successful human capital consulting firms, an as executive of a multi-million dollar leadership consulting firm, and as a leading researcher and author known throughout the Fortune 500 as a cutting-edge thinker in the area of trends in executive development and identifying and developing high-potential and emerging leaders.

Prior to JMP, Mattone was the Vice President of Global Assessment Services for Linkage, Inc., where he was responsible for the firm's global assessment practice. Prior to Linkage, John Mattone was the Senior Vice President of Sales for Drake Beam Morin, the global career and outplacement firm. Before joining DBM, Mattone spent 10 years building his first successful consulting firm, Human Resources International.

John Mattone has consulted for more than 250 organizations, and addressed more than 500,000 people in 2,000 speeches and seminars throughout the U.S., Canada, and other countries worldwide. John is a prolific author, having written seven books as well as more than 100 professional articles and book chapters including the award-winning "The Role of Assessment in Driving Operating Results," published in Jac Fitz-enz's book *The New HR Analytics* (AMACOM, 2010) and "Predictive HR Leadership." John's newest books, *Talent Leadership: A Proven Method for Identifying and Developing High-Potential Employees* and *Intelligent Leadership: What You Need to Know to Unlock Your Full Potential* (Foreword by Marshall Goldsmith), are being heralded by leading experts, CEOs, and HR leaders as "groundbreaking and innovative."

Mattone holds a B.S. degree in Management and Organizational Behavior from Babson College, and an M.S. degree in Industrial/Organizational Psychology from the University of Central Florida. He serves as an Executive MBA faculty member at Florida Atlantic University, where he teaches his popular course "Global Leadership Assessment & Development." He is also an adjunct faculty member at the Owen School of Management at Vanderbilt University. Mattone also serves as a Senior Talent Management Consultant and Master Executive Coach for Executive Development Associates (where he also served as President) and as a Senior Faculty Member with the Talent Management

Academy, a worldwide leader in leadership conferences and education. John Mattone is a member of numerous professional associations including the Society for Industrial and Organizational Psychology, and is certified as a Master Corporate Executive Coach™ (MCEC) by the Association of Corporate Executive Coaches.

For More Information:

Jan Jones, President
Jan Jones Worldwide Speakers Bureau
Tel: +1-760-431-8692 • Fax: +1-760-431-6791
Email: Jan@JanJonesWorldwide.com

CPSIA information can be obtained
at www.ICGtesting.com
Printed in the USA
BVHW030010301018
531635BV00001B/50/P